Angelsong

Joan Vibert

DEDICATION

This book is dedicated to daughters and sisters. They are the angels in our lives—treasure them.

ACKNOWLEDGMENTS

Angelsong might never have been written were it not for Karen Oversteadt and Pam Fowler. Karen co-owns the local quilt shop and steered me through a blind panic when time started running out. Pam is my own personal angel. She volunteered to make quilts within a schedule that would have discouraged anyone. Pam made both Snowstar quilts from my sparse, colored-pencil drawings. After seeing the dolls, she worked up the Angels around the World Quilt, machine appliqued the Pageant Time Quilt, and thought of putting the Guardian Angel on a stocking with the crib, after I had looked at the design for several months and couldn't find a use for it. During all of this, Pam kept me sane.

CREDITS

Photography . . . . Carl Murray
Brent Kane
Illustration and Graphics . . . . Barb Tourtillotte
Text and Cover Design . . . . Judy Petry
Editorial . . . . Liz McGehee

Angelsong©

Printed in the United States of America
96 95 94 93 92 91 90 89 6 5 4 3 2 1

Library of Congress Cataloging-in-Publication Data

Vibert, Joan, 1941-
Angelsong / Joan Vibert.
p. cm.
ISBN 0-943574-57-9
1. Quilting--Patterns. 2. Christmas decorations. 3. Angels in art. I. Title.
TT835.V52 1989 88-51648
746.46--dc20 CIP

Be not forgetful to entertain strangers: for thereby some have entertained angels unawares. BOOK OF HEBREWS (13:2)

Contents

Introduction

I started Angelsong in the fall of 1987 after attending Quilt Market in Houston. Antique Santas had reached their pinnacle that year, and I had been overwhelmed by all of them at the show. Through conversations with my roommates there, Donna Gallagher and Becky Tuttle, I had begun to see that others were feeling the same way. I left feeling a need for something cleaner and simpler, and with Christmas coming, I was ready to tackle a new theme.

Charlotte Hagood, who was with *Creative Ideas for Living* magazine and is now at Oxmoor House, and I started sharing ideas and observations from what we had seen. Rarely have I ever been so excited and inspired. It all began to come together in my head.

Throughout that last day, I tried to draw up some ideas and I couldn't wait to get into the car the next morning. My husband, Jim, had flown down to drive back with me, and after one look at my face, he knew I would be of no help with the driving. Angels were dancing in my head!

I began to draw angels. Quilted, stuffed, or ornaments—it didn't matter—I wanted to make every one of them now! I always travel with fabric and my sewing box. By the time we got home, I had finished most of the Angelsong quilt and begun several of the ornaments.

I knew why I was so excited. Angels remind me of children, and by working with angels, I had allowed myself to return to my very favorite subject: childhood. Children have the glorious ability to see right through the superfluous and reach the spirit. Only adults who have left imagination behind, insist upon the superficial trappings to create angels. No gauzy, filmy, sequined fabric is necessary to create an angel. Take a sheet, cut wings from corrugated cardboard, and any child becomes an angel.

All the angels and projects in this book are fun, simple designs inspired by children. I hope you enjoy making them.

General Instructions

Basic Sewing Supplies

Template plastic: Templates made from plastic are easier to work with and are permanent. You will want to use plastic that is clear enough to see through and will hold a pencil line.

Quilting needles: I recommend Betweens sizes 7, 8, 9, or 10. The shorter the needle used, the more control you will have. I use a quilting needle not only for quilting, but also for hand piecing and applique.

Embroidery needles: Be sure to have several sizes, to accommodate one to six strands of embroidery floss.

Craft needles: You will want to have various sizes. One should have an eye large enough to thread a 1/16″ ribbon through.

Thimble: Invest in a good one that fits well on your middle finger, so you will always wear it. This is a most important habit to form.

Straight pins: You will need both quilting length and regular length ones. I use pins with glass heads because they show up on the carpet and furniture.

Cotton mercerized thread: I use cotton for hand piecing and applique because it does not tangle like polyester. You can also use cotton for quilting, but it should be well waxed.

Quilting thread: You will want to use this thread for hand quilting.

Scissors: You will want two pairs, one good-quality pair for cutting fabric only and one for cutting templates.

Rulers: A small, transparent gridded ruler is handy, but you will also want a yardstick or longer ruler.

Lead pencil: You can use this pencil for marking light fabrics. It should be a soft, #2 pencil, sharpened to a fine point for accurate lines.

White pencil: You will need white for marking dark fabrics. The best I have found is a Berol Verithin™. It will hold a point well and doesn't break easily.

Seam ripper: There is no substitute for this tool when you need it. It is faster and less damaging than other methods.

Beeswax: Waxing your thread keeps it from knotting as you sew by hand.

OPTIONAL SEWING SUPPLIES
(things I wouldn't want to do without!)

Rotary cutter and pad: My favorite pad is gridded, making it easy to keep fabric square when cutting.

Gridded ruler for rotary cutter: This ruler should be 24″ long, so that it covers a width of folded fabric.

Glue gun: I am a recent convert to this tool, and I must admit it beats holding two pieces together while waiting for the glue to dry. Just be very careful and follow manufacturer's directions when using.

Fabric

The fabric used for all of the projects in this book, unless otherwise specified, is 42″–45″ wide and 100 percent cotton. I highly recommend that you wash all fabrics prior to starting any project.

The yardages given for each project may seem excessive, since often scraps of fabrics will suffice. However, for those of you not blessed with a cupboard full of scraps, I have included the amounts you will need to purchase in order to complete each project.

Color Selection

Some of the quilts have been made with nontraditional Christmas colors. I found myself pulling out the blue-greens instead of just green, going to a pinky floral print to stand in for red, and when red was used, I chose brown rather than green to go with it. Since many homes have gone to the softer pastel colors, I see no reason to make up a tree skirt in red and green and lay it on top of apricot-colored carpet. If you are going to go to all of the work involved in making a quilt or table cover and then live with it for perhaps a month, why not use colors that will complement your color scheme? Very few of the fabrics used were originally purchased for Christmas projects, but they work and add their own interest to the designs. Since many of these quilts are small and do not require a great amount of time to complete, they are ideal for being adventurous with different colors.

I often dye many of the fabrics I use to tone them down or mellow them. Most bright or light fabrics will take well to Rit™ tan dye. You can dye up to three yards of 100 percent cotton fabric at one time with one box of Rit™. I use a sixteen-quart, graniteware preserving kettle. To dye fabric, fill the pot two-thirds full of water and bring it to a low boil. Reduce heat to low, add one box of dye, and stir until dissolved. Add fabric, stirring well after each addition. You can dye several fabrics at once, as long as you do not exceed a total of three yards. You will need to watch carefully and stir often to distribute the dye throughout the fabric. Most dyeing will take twenty to thirty minutes, but some fabrics will reach the desired color in five minutes. Just remember your fabric will be lighter when dry. Rinse fabric well, squeeze (don't wring), and dry.

A second choice for altering fabric is bleaching, which produces a soft and faded look. However, bleaching is less predictable than dye and is best left to your washing machine. Add a cup of chlorine bleach to a washer full of hot water. Agitate for a minute and then add fabric, up to three yards. Agitate continuously for several minutes. Check fabric, remembering that it will be lighter when dry. You may wish to reset the time for further agitation; up to thirty minutes won't hurt. Drain fabric and run through the wash cycle with soap to remove the chlorine odor; dry. You may alter very small amounts of fabric in a mixing bowl or even a large cup by reducing the amounts of dye or bleach proportionately.

Of course, we all know what a wonderful mellowing job the sun can do on fabric. It is somewhat less damaging than bleach but does require patience!

Backing

Backing fabric is an area that is largely ignored. Often, there is a tendency to slap on some muslin and consider it done. Maybe so much of our energy goes into choosing the fabrics for the front of the quilt that we take a line of least resistance for the back. This is a place for fun! Bizarre fabrics can be used, in some cases, very successfully, or try a novelty print. At the very least, you could use up some of your old fabrics or ones that haven't worked anywhere else. The back can be pieced together in "make-do" fashion for a primitive quilt. Give yourself a challenge and see how many quilts you can make without a muslin backing.

Batting

For the smaller quilts in this book, I did not use batting and instead finished them with a No-Bind backing method (see the Binding section on page 8). An alternate method would be to use cotton flannel, which gives a tiny amount of body to a quilt. I prefer a flat batting, such as Fairfield's Traditional Needlepunch or Cotton Classic. (Cotton Classic should be used only if the piece will be closely quilted or never washed, since it does not hold together well when washed. Quilting should be no farther than 2″ apart over the entire quilt, if you plan to wash a quilt made with this batting.) The batting is always cut to the finished size of the quilt, except in quilts with extensive hand quilting (see Quilting section on page 8).

Sewing the Projects

This section contains instructions for methods that are used throughout the book. The individual instructions given with each project only cover methods or sequences particular to that project. Always sew fabrics with right sides together, unless otherwise stated.

TEMPLATES

Some pattern pieces are printed on the pull-out pattern section, stapled in the center of the book. Open staple to remove pages; reclose staple to keep book intact. Store pattern pieces in a large manila envelope glued to inside back cover.

The pattern pieces in this book should be transferred to template material. I prefer template plastic because it is permanent. Cardboard has a tendency to "shrink" each time it is drawn around and retains the lead from the pencil on its edges to get all over your hands. Tracing paper is flimsy and tiny pieces are hard to pin and cut around. Flat sculpture and soft sculpture all use the trace, stitch, and cut technique, so the pattern pieces are the finished size. Seam allowances are added as you cut out the pattern pieces, using this sequence:

1. Fold fabric in half with right sides together. Trace pattern pieces and markings from template onto wrong side of fabric.
2. Sew pieces together, stitching directly on the drawn line and leaving an opening for turning.
3. Cut off excess fabric ¼″ from stitching line. Clip curves.

Clothing for angels uses conventional patterns with ¼″ seam allowance. For applique projects, trace around the templates on the right side of fabric with a sharp, soft lead pencil, or white pencil on dark fabrics. All other craft projects in this book require you to trace the templates on the wrong side of the fabric, unless otherwise stated. You can also use a Pilot SC-UF™ pen to draw around templates; however, do not use normal felt-tip or ball-point pens. A sheet of very fine sand-paper placed under the fabric will keep the fabric from slipping when you are tracing.

Templates for pieced quilts include the ¼″ seam allowance and should be made according to the piecing technique that you will be using. You will find specific directions under Quilt Piecing below.

Portions of some projects, such as quilt borders or angel skirts, have measurements instead of templates. These measurements are the actual size to be cut and include the ¼″ seam allowance.

QUILT PIECING

For hand piecing, cut out all pattern pieces and mark the ¼″ seam allowance. This line is your sewing line. Place two pieces together and match up with a pin in each corner of the sewing line. Several pins placed along the line will keep the two pieces lined up. Stitch, using a backstitch at the beginning and end of each seam instead of a knot. Check the other side occasionally to make sure that the two seams are lining up. Leave all seam allowances free when assembling; do not sew over a seam allowance.

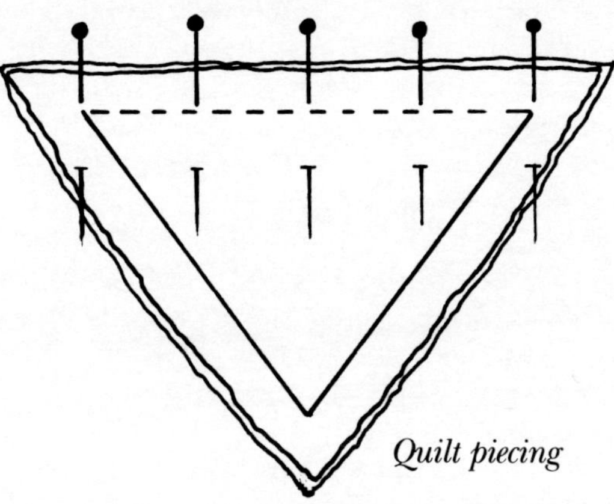

Quilt piecing

For machine piecing, cut fabrics, match up the cut edges, and pin. Make sure that your pressure foot is a true ¼″; then sew seam, using the pressure foot as a gauge. You can sew over seam allowances unless they are at a point where the sewing direction is pivoting or changing.

APPLIQUE

For hand applique, add ¼″ seam allowance before you cut out all pattern pieces. You can merely estimate this amount, and on very small pieces, you can reduce the seam allowance to 3⁄16″ or even ⅛″. Baste appliques in position on the background piece. Clip inside curves only. Turn under seam allowance to the pencil line, smoothing it under with the needle and turning ahead only ½″–1″. Hold turned under section in place with thumb and, using a quilting needle, applique with very small blind stitches. A small tug after each stitch will bring the applique flush with the background. Template numbers identify each applique piece and indicate the order in which they are to be sewn. Be sure to applique each piece in the correct sequence or you will find yourself taking out stitches to tuck in other pieces.

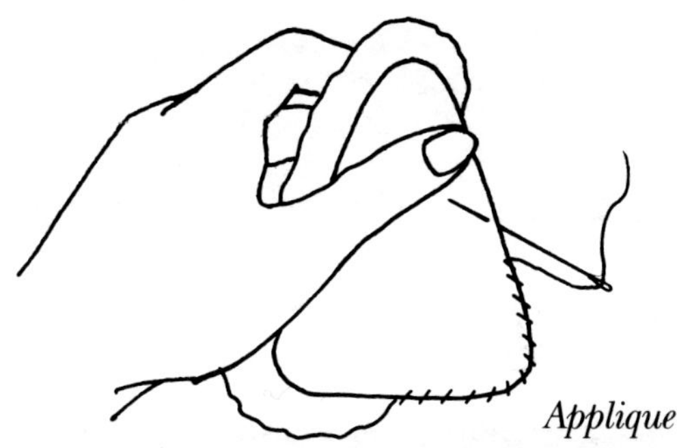

Applique

When appliqueing narrow areas, do not baste down the center of the narrow section. Baste the main part of the applique with stitches that are separate from the narrow section. Baste the narrow section along one side only in the seam allowance. Applique the side opposite your basting and, as you come around to the basted side, remove the basting before appliqueing.

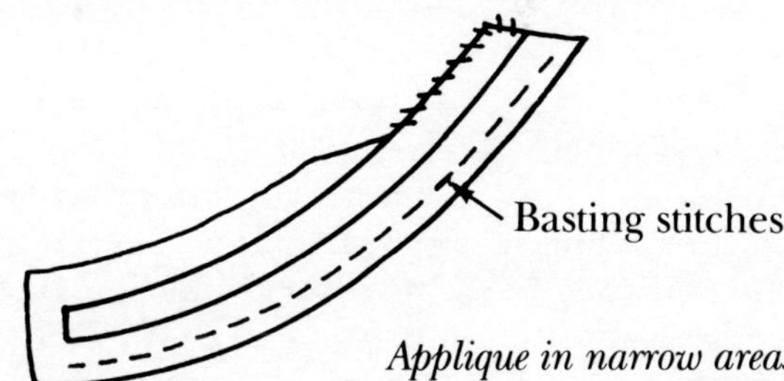

Applique in narrow areas

For machine applique, do not add seam allowance before cutting out pieces. Use a glue stick or Wonder-Under™, a fusible webbing, to hold pieces in position. Sew around each applique piece with a narrow, close zigzag stitch, using thread to match the applique fabric.

Wonder-Under™ has absolutely refined quick appliques. It has a paper backing, which you can trace on before ironing it to the fabric. Trace on all of the applique patterns needed, keeping in mind that you are tracing them in reverse. Leave room between patterns to cut them apart. Cut apart and, following manufacturer's directions, iron onto wrong side of desired fabrics. By doing this, you don't have to guess how much fabric you will need to cover. Cut out fabric appliques on the drawn lines, remove the paper backing, and position appliques on the background fabric. Again, follow manufacturer's directions for final ironing. At this point you have several options. You can machine stitch the appliques, you can work around the appliques by hand with a buttonhole stitch, or you can leave the appliques as they are. For a quick and simple wall hanging, ironing on the appliques is sufficient. The project cannot be washed and should be rolled up to store instead of folding, but, with a minimum of effort, you have a decoration that can provide years of enjoyment.

ASSEMBLING THE QUILT TOP

After sewing the quilt top together, carefully iron it, pressing all seams to the darker side. Do not iron appliques. To assemble the quilt top with backing and batting, lay your backing flat, wrong side facing up; lay batting over it; then finished quilt top, facing up. Smooth all three layers with your hands and baste layers together.

QUILTING

Quilt-as-you-go frames can be used on smaller quilts. If you plan to use a hoop or will be doing extensive hand quilting, it is a good idea to leave about 6″ of backing and batting beyond the edges of the quilt top. Baste right to the edge of the quilt top. You can then easily quilt close to the outside edges of the quilt when it is in a hoop.

Place quilt in a hoop or frame. Smooth both top and backing. The quilt should be loose enough to be able to move up and down freely. All quilting should begin in the center and work toward the sides. Use quilting thread or mercerized thread, which has been drawn through beeswax, and a quilting needle. Do not double the thread; put a small knot in one end of it. Starting about ½″ from where you plan to quilt, take a stitch through the top layer only, emerging at the desired starting point. Pop the knot into the fabric to hide it. Quilt with small, even running stitches through all three layers. Do not quilt over basting stitches; take them out when you come to them. The most natural direction for quilting is toward your body. If you keep your thread no longer than 18″, you will minimize your arm movements and thus be able to quilt for a longer period of time.

TYING A QUILT

A homey alternative to quilting is tying your quilt, with or without batting. If you are not using batting, then use the No-Bind backing method (see Binding section on this page). Using embroidery floss in a pleasant contrasting color, thread an embroidery needle, and take a small stitch from the front of the quilt, through all layers, leaving a 2″ tail on each side. Tie floss in a square knot and trim ends to about 1″. Tying is usually done at the junction of two corners or in an area that won't conflict with the pattern, such as in the center of a pieced square.

Tying a quilt

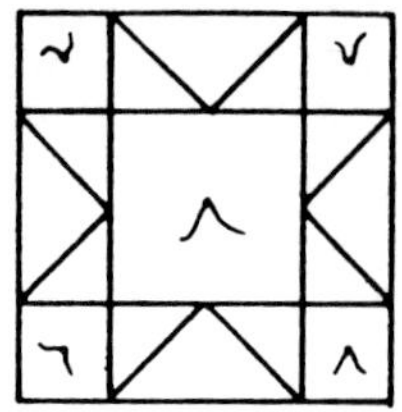

Tie in areas that don't conflict with pattern

BINDING

No-Bind backing is what I call the finishing method for quilts without batting. Cut backing fabric to the same size as assembled quilt top. With right sides together, sew around outside edge, leaving a 2″ opening at lower center. Trim corners and turn; press. Blindstitch opening closed.

Another simple binding method is to turn the backing fabric over the front and blindstitch down. Trim the batting even with the front and trim the backing ½″ larger all the way around. Fold the backing under ¼″, pull to the front, and blindstitch down.

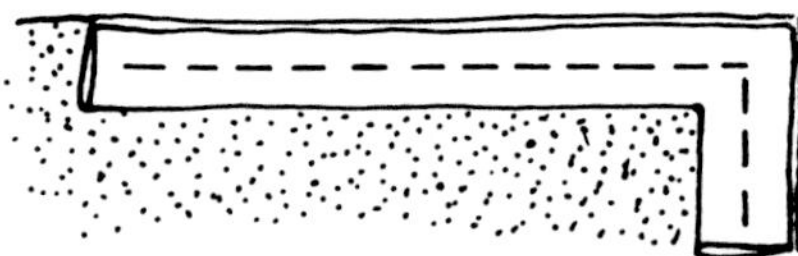

On small quilts, you can sew 2″ crosswise-cut strips end to end to make the binding. With wrong sides together, press in half lengthwise. Trim the backing and batting even with the front. Matching raw edges of the strip with raw edges of the quilt, sew onto front of quilt with a ¼″ seam. Where the two ends of the binding meet, turn under the end ¼″ and slightly overlap the beginning raw end of the binding. Blindstitch the two sections together. Pull folded edge to the back and slip-stitch down.

On larger quilts, I recommend bias binding; it is much easier to work with. Apply it in the same fashion as I described for the smaller quilts. To make continuous binding:

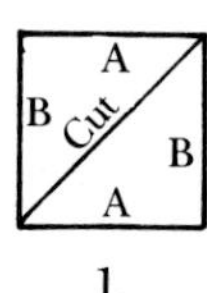

2. (diagram: A, A)

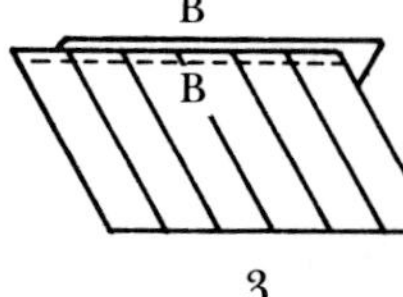

1. Cut a 27″ x 27″ square of desired fabric. Label as shown in diagram. Cut on the diagonal.
2. With A lines right sides together, sew ½″ seams, overlapping the points. On the wrong side of fabric, mark 2″ widths and join the marks with a straight line.

3. Bring B lines together with marked lines to the outside. Leave one bias width at each end. Sew together as shown.
4. Cut on marked lines in one continuous strip. This will give you six yards of bias binding.

STUFFED SOFT SCULPTURE

All of the three-dimensional stuffed projects in this book, unless otherwise stated, are sewn prior to cutting them out. I have utilized this method for years, and it simplifies the sewing of small shapes, which otherwise never seem to line up for me. Simply trace your templates on fabric that has been folded with right sides together. Leave room between pieces for ¼″ seam allowances. Sew on drawn line, leaving an opening, as indicated on the pattern. Cut out pieces, clipping any inside curves, and turn. After stuffing, slip-stitch opening closed.

Stuffing is easier and more uniform if you use very small tufts of stuffing, about the size of a walnut. Fluff each piece by pulling it apart several times before inserting it into the item. This is very important. I have actually seen people roll stuffing between their hands and then cram it into a doll's head. This method produces nothing but lumps of stuffing that never mesh with neighboring lumps. A stuffing tool that I would never be without is a pencil length of ¼″ diameter wood doweling that has been slightly sharpened in a pencil sharpener. This tool directs the stuffing much nicer than your finger and is invaluable for narrow or long areas. Polyester stuffing is recommended.

When embroidering stuffed objects, such as a face, I prefer to do it after I stuff the item. Invariably, when I embroider before stuffing, it is never quite right. By waiting, I take advantage of seeing the full shape before sewing on the face. You can sew fine, delicate faces with a single strand of embroidery floss or mercerized thread and a quilting needle.

FLAT SCULPTURE

Many times, I prefer a flatter look than what stuffing an object gives, so I will merely use batting. Garlands, ornaments, and wall decorations all fit into this category. Place two fabrics, with right sides together, and trace around your template onto the top fabric. Place the fabrics over a piece of batting and pin all three layers together. Sew on drawn line, leaving an opening as indicated on the pattern. Cut out, clip inside curves, and turn. Slip-stitch opening closed.

COUNTED CROSS-STITCH

This needle art is done on even-weave fabric, which is available in 11, 14, 18, and 22 threads per inch and a wide variety of colors and textures. A tapestry needle and six-strand cotton embroidery floss complete the short list of necessary items. The thread count of your fabric determines the size of the needle and number of strands of floss to use. The lower the thread count, the more strands of floss and the larger the needle. Using masking tape, tape your fabric along all cut edges to prevent further unraveling.

Different symbols on the cross-stitch charts indicate each color used. The Xs indicate stitches worked across your fabric from left to right on the first pass and right to left on the return pass. Each time, the stitches all go the same direction (see illustration).

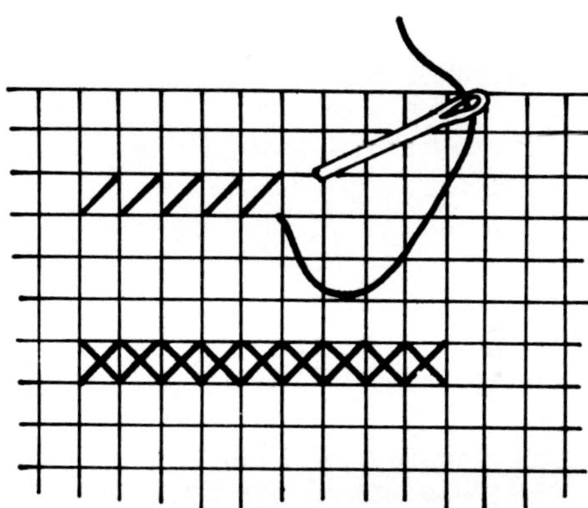

Counted cross-stitch

Cut your fabric several inches larger than the design size. The floss should be cut no longer than 18″ and separated into the correct number of strands. Find the center of your fabric by folding and start working the design by counting from the center. The center of the design is marked along the sides of the chart. With your first stitch, leave a 1″ tail on the back, stitching over it as you work the first row. On light-colored fabric, do not carry your thread between designs, as it will show. When changing thread, you can work the ending tail under stitches on the back.

PERFORATED PAPER

This is a revival of an old medium for needle art. I have used it for projects as if it were even-weave fabric. The look is well worth the extra effort involved in handling. Perforated paper is quite stiff and somewhat fragile. It is available in brown 9″ x 12″ craft paper sheets with fourteen holes to the inch. These sheets can be cut to the sizes needed. Carefully read the instructions that are provided with the paper. Since cross-stitch fabric holds the needle, it was very disconcerting to have my needle fall out with each stitch, as soon as I brought my hand to the top side. Thus, I have found that a slightly larger tapestry needle, which fits almost snugly in the holes, is best to use. Use three strands of floss. You do not need to fill in the background areas, so the work goes quickly.

FABRIC PAINTING

The paints used for decorative fabric painting are the liquid artist's acrylic paints found in most quilt and craft stores. These come in handy squeeze bottles so that you can squirt out just a dab at a time. A dab is all you need, since the paint drys very quickly, in thirty minutes or less. Textile medium, added to the paint in equal parts, makes the coverage more satisfactory and the fabric washable, if heat-set according to manufacturer's directions.

You need only a small assortment of brushes: a ½″ or ¾″ wide brush for base coating, a ¼″ wide chisel edge brush for small areas or narrow lines, and a small, round-pointed brush for dots and detail. You can easily wash these with liquid soap and water and reuse them before they dry, as long as you shake out the excess water from them. Put only a small amount of paint on your brush at one time; don't try to load it up or you will only drive the paint up into the bristles and make it difficult to clean the brush. When the brushes are washed and ready to store, be sure to shape them so they will dry in that position.

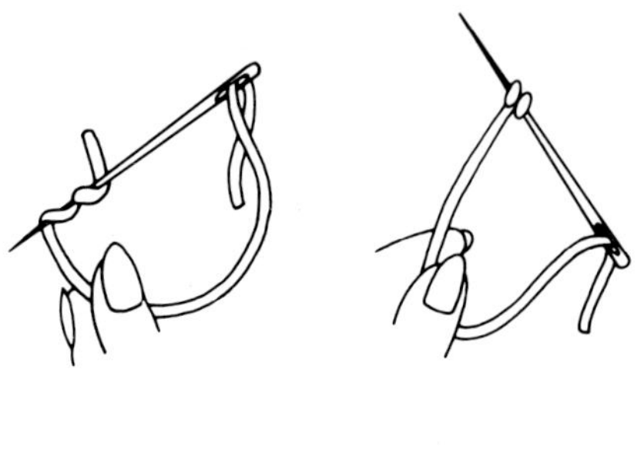

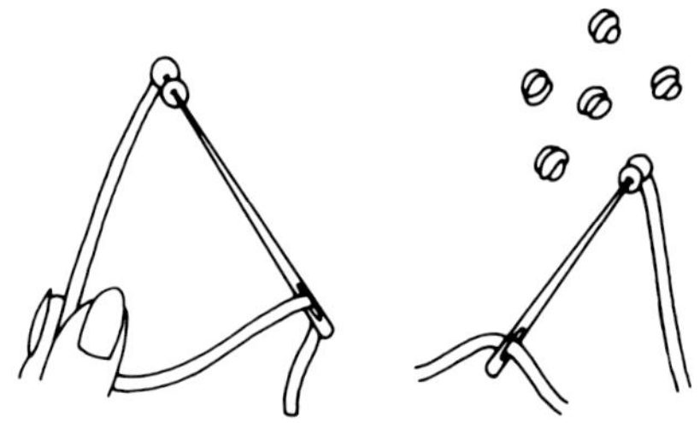

French knot

EMBROIDERY

Embroidery adds detail or finishing touches to many of the projects in this book. I use embroidery needles and embroidery floss for most of these projects. The smaller the needle, the finer the stitch you will achieve. I normally use two strands of embroidery floss; however, a single strand in a small needle will produce a very delicate line. For larger eyes, you can use three, or even six, strands of floss and make **French knots**.

The **satin stitch** is good for filling in an area, such as round eyes. You can use the **outline stitch** for lines, such as mouths. I have used the **straight stitch** for hair on the Angelsong ornaments. Use the **buttonhole stitch** to finish the edges of iron-on appliques. Follow the appropriate stitch diagram and make small, accurate stitches.

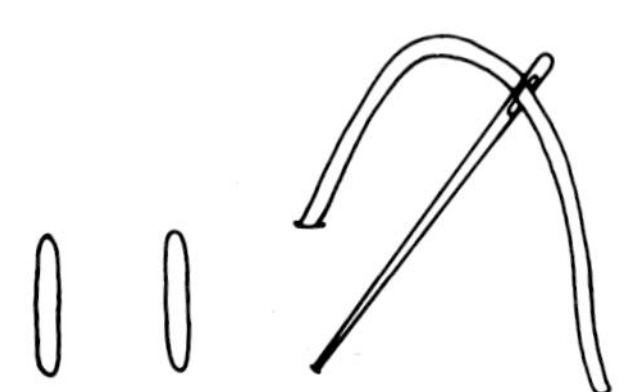

Straight stitch

Outline stitch

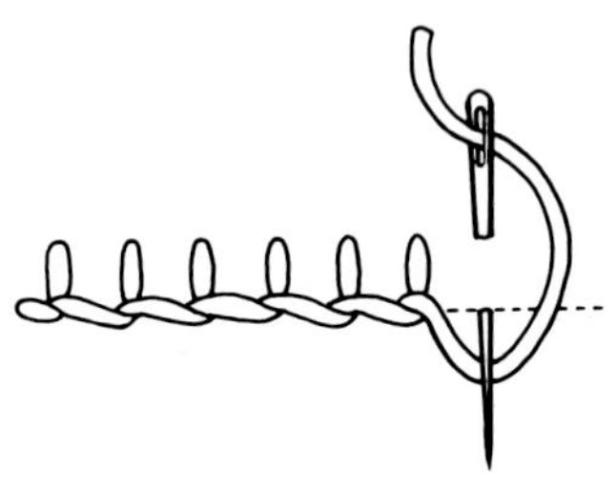

Buttonhole stitch

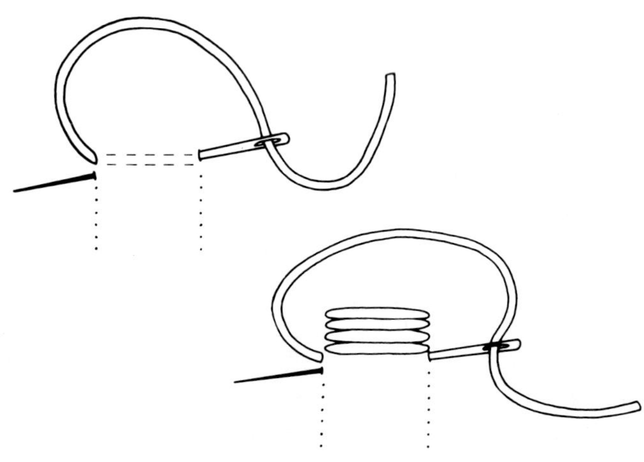

Satin stitch

Angelsong

CARL MURRAY

CARL MURRAY

An Angelsong Quilt (left) made from a variety of homespun plaids and prints hangs next to a small tree decorated with Angelsong Ornaments. The ribbon from each side of the Angelsong Ornaments can be tied together to form a garland. Detail of Angelsong Ornament (above).

These primitive little angels remind me of children's drawings. The little "o" mouths, open in joyful song, create such an innocent look. The childlike feel is why I used the red and brown combination in the quilt. Having watched small children color, I know that the actual colors used are often not as important to them as coloring the object and finishing it. It's not until later that the selection of colors becomes a part of the process. The fabric used in this quilt was perfect for achieving the scrap look, while still keeping the same overall colors.

I cut the little Angelsong ornaments from the only quilt I have ever cut. It was very worn and not particularly well sewn or well planned, but still it distressed me to cut into it. I don't intend to cut into an uncut quilt ever again. It is much easier on my conscience to age and soften new fabrics and a whole lot kinder to our heritage of old quilts. Even a homely one keeps you warm!

Angelsong Quilt

11¼″ x 13½″

MATERIALS

⅛ yd. each of 2 brown prints for background squares
⅛ yd. red and brown plaid for background squares
⅛ yd. each of 9 different light prints for wings
⅛ yd. each of 9 different red prints for dresses and first border
⅛ yd. muslin for faces
⅛ yd. brown homespun plaid for outer border
⅜ yd. fabric for backing
Black embroidery floss

DIRECTIONS

1. Cut 9 background squares. Cut out and position appliques onto background squares; applique.
2. Embroider faces with a French knot for eyes and an outline stitch for mouths. Stitch hair as for Angelsong Ornaments on this page.
3. Following picture for placement, sew background squares together.
4. From red print, cut 2 strips 1″ x 11″ and 2 strips 1″ x 10¼″. Sew longer strips to sides of quilt and shorter strips to top and bottom. From brown homespun, cut 2 strips 1½″ x 12″ and 2 strips 1½″ x 11¾″ for border. Sew as before.
5. Finish quilt with a No-Bind backing (see page 8 for instructions).

Angelsong Ornaments

3½″ tall

You can make these individual ornaments into a garland by merely untying the bows and retying each angel's ribbons together.

MATERIALS

⅛ yd. soft blue print or old quilt pieces
⅛ yd. brown print or old quilt pieces
⅛ yd. white print or old quilt pieces
⅛ yd. pink for heads
⅛ yd. muslin, if using quilt pieces
Black embroidery floss
Batting (not needed if using old quilt pieces)
Polyester stuffing
2½ yds. cream satin ribbon, 1/16″ wide

DIRECTIONS

1. If not using old quilt pieces, use the Flat Sculpture method (see page 9) to sew 5 bodies and 5 wings. Pattern pieces are found on page 13. If you use quilt pieces, omit the layer of batting and use muslin for the backing fabric, if desired, to make the quilt pieces go further.
2. Sew, cut out, and turn 5 heads; stuff lightly. Place these over stem of neck, turn under seam, and sew to body. Place wings behind body and tack to body at top and bottom of center wing.
3. Sew faces with a small outline stitch and a single strand of embroidery floss. The eyes are tiny French knots and the hair is just a continuous stitch taken over the center head seam.

Sewing hair

4. Thread a large-eyed needle with 7½″ of ribbon, which has been knotted at 1 end. Sew through the point of the wing from the back to the front. Tie a knot close to the fabric on the front. Repeat for all wings.
5. Tie ribbons into a bow above each head or tie bows together to form a garland.

ANGELSONG QUILT

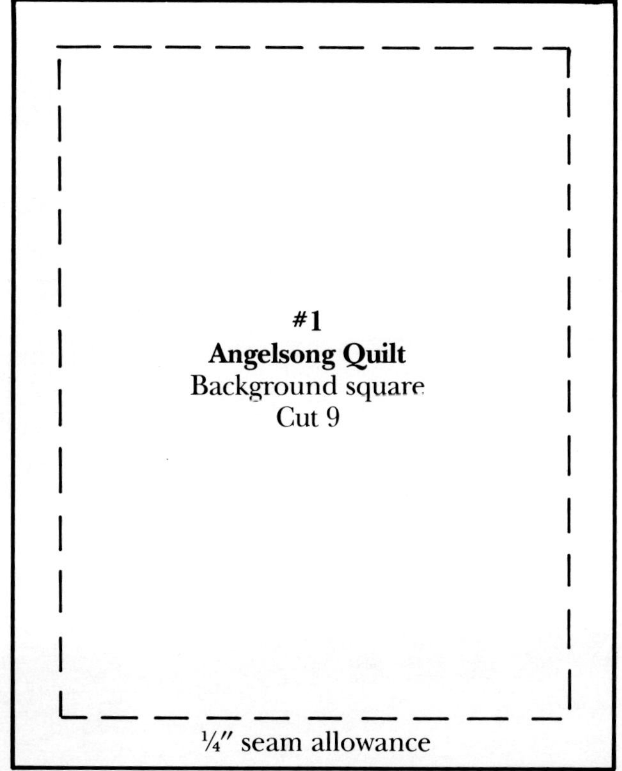

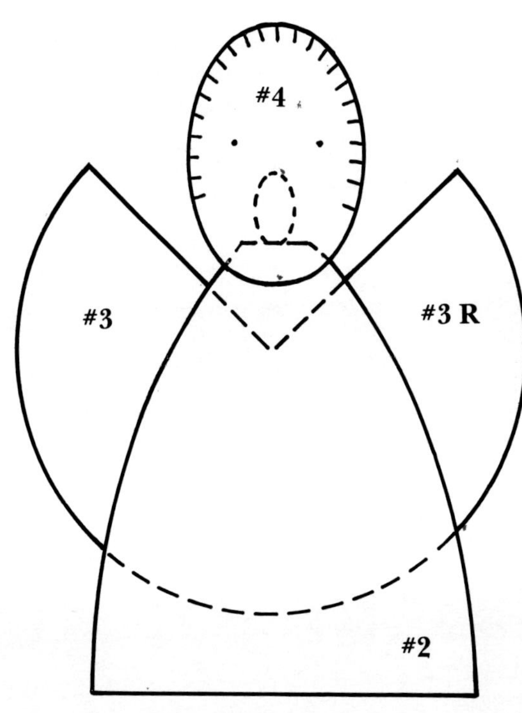

ANGELSONG GARLAND AND ORNAMENT

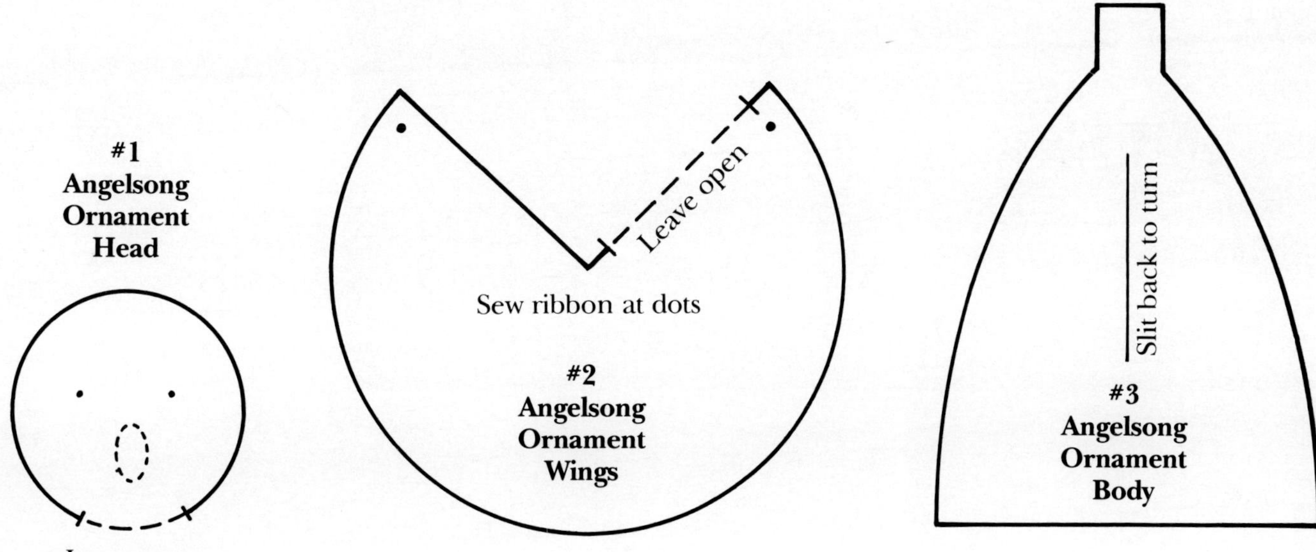

Christmas Is Memories

BRENT KANE

BRENT KANE

The Pageant Time Quilt (above) brings back childhood memories of the annual Christmas pageant. Christmas Is a Child's Face Quilt (left) combines both cross-stitch and applique.

BRENT KANE

You have probably noticed that most of the angels in this book either have no faces or childlike faces. When I think of angels, I think of children. When I was young, our parents made us a stage in the basement, where we put on shows. The highlight of our year was our annual Christmas Show, which was truly an extravaganza, as I remember it. A major conflict always occurred, because we all wanted to be angels. So, we had several years of an "All-Angel Variety Show." We all performed our specialties and our patient parents tried not to laugh too loud. I can still see my brother, Rocky, at the age of three, wrapped in a sheet with his bow tie peeking out, singing "Away in a Manger."

Lizzie (caught in her underwear!) sits amidst sewing notions and two cross-stitch designs. Christmas Is a Child's Face is done on perforated paper and features treasured children's photos. Christmas Is Memories is stitched on 14-count Aida cloth.

Christmas Is Memories Cross-Stitch

4½″ x 6½″

MATERIALS

7″ x 10″, 14 ct. ivory Aida
Green, pink, gold, blue, and brown embroidery floss (see chart)
Purchased mat and frame

DIRECTIONS

1. Cut Aida 7″ x 10″ and tape edges. Using chart found on pages 20 and 21 as a guide to stitching and color placement, cross-stitch design on Aida.
2. Mount into purchased mat and frame. Sample shown in photo is mounted in a double 8″ x 10″ mat with 4½″ x 6½″ opening inside a 8″ x 10″ wood frame. Size and color of mat and frame may be varied to suit your holiday decor.

Christmas Is a Child's Face Cross-Stitch

9″ x 13″

The photographs you use do not have to be photocopies, but I prefer the look of black and white. Small school pictures are just the right size for this, but if reducing is necessary, you should have no problem finding a copier that will reduce them. If your copy store offers brown ink, you might want to try that for a real antique look!

MATERIALS

9″ x 12″ sheet of perforated paper
Red, green, white, and black embroidery floss (see chart)
Children's small photographs, photocopied and reduced, if desired
Glue
Purchased mat and frame

DIRECTIONS

1. Cut perforated paper to 7″ x 12″. (The strip you cut off is perfect for the bookmarks.) Following chart found on pages 22 and 23 and using 3 strands of embroidery floss, complete cross-stitch design.
2. In each of the small framed sections of paper, cut an opening. Cut along the next row of holes beyond the stitching. Cut out photocopy to fit just behind black frame, so that it doesn't extend beyond. Lightly glue in place; too much glue will ooze through the openings. Repeat for other 3 openings.
3. Mount into purchased mat and frame. Size and color of mat and frame may be varied to suit your holiday decor.

Christmas Is a Child's Face Quilt

20½″ x 12¼″

MATERIALS

¼ yd. blue print for background
¼ yd. red print for dress, shirt, and binding
⅛ yd. stripe for top and bottom borders
⅛ yd. soft yellow for hair and wings
⅛ yd. pink for faces and hands
⅛ yd. gold print for pants
⅛ yd. black for shoes
⅜ yd. fabric for backing
Black and red embroidery floss (see chart)
10″ x 12″, 14 ct. ivory Aida
Batting

DIRECTIONS

1. Cross-stitch the words only for center motif, using chart on pages 22 and 23 as a guide. Trim completed motif to 7⅜″ x 8¾″.
2. Cut 2 background squares 7⅜″ x 8¾″. Using patterns found on page 19, cut out and position appliques on squares; applique, noting correct sequence. Embroider faces with French knots and use black embroidery floss to outline stitch boy's pants.
3. Sew appliqued squares to either side of cross-stitched motif.
4. Cut 2 border strips 2½″ x 21″. Sew to top and bottom of quilt.
5. Layer quilt with backing and batting; baste. Outline quilt around appliques and ⅛″ from border and center seams.
6. Bind with red print.

Lizzie (caught in her underwear!)

12″ tall

While researching angels, I was struck by the fact that so many of the angels from the turn of the century were merely children with wings attached. They were dressed in coats and hats, and the little girls even carried muffs. The boys wore shorts and little sailor suits. So, I reasoned, if angels wore everyday type clothes, why not catch them in their underwear? And this is what happened to Lizzie, in her little pantaloons and camisole.

MATERIALS

¼ yd. muslin for body and clothes
⅛ yd. tan solid for hair
½ yd. ecru lace with center ribbon channel
1½ yds. cream satin ribbon, 1/16″ wide
Tan, pale green, and pink embroidery floss
Polyester stuffing
Batting for wings
Fabric glue

DIRECTIONS

1. Using patterns found on pages 24 and 25, assemble body, head, arms, and legs with trace, stitch, and cut technique (see page 9); stuff. Insert arms and legs into openings, turn under raw edges of body fabric, and sew with a running stitch through all layers. Place head over neck, turn under raw edge of head opening, and blindstitch to body.
2. Trace around hair onto folded piece of tan fabric. Sew entire outline. Cut out with ⅛″ seam; clip curves and corners. Cut a small slit in the center, as drawn, through 1 layer only; turn. Place on back of head and bring bangs over center seam onto forehead. Blindstitch main part of hair to center seam of head and bangs to forehead.
3. Embroider face with a single strand of embroidery floss. Satin stitch eyes and use a long single stitch for eyelashes. Outline stitch nose and mouth.
4. Cut pantaloons and camisole from muslin. Sew side and shoulder seams of camisole. Turn under armholes and sew with a running stitch. Turn under neck edge and sew with a running stitch, using 15″ of ribbon in a large-eyed needle. Leave equal length tails at beginning and end.
5. Sew side and inseams of pantaloons. Turn under waist and sew, using 13″ of ribbon in a large-eyed needle; leave tails. Cut 2 pieces of lace, each 4½″ long, and sew to bottom of leg openings. Thread 13″ long pieces of ribbon through the channels in lace.
6. Dress doll in camisole and pantaloons and tie bows at neck, waist, and legs.
7. Sew wings as for Flat Sculpture (see page 9). Cut the rest of the lace in half lengthwise and sew to front edge of wings. Glue wings to back of angel.

Pageant Time Quilt

48″ x 28″

This quilt contains all the elements I remember from my school days:

The little red-haired girl in front desperately wanted a new dress for the pageant, but instead is forced to wear an old, faded brown one, which was scrubbed clean, freshly starched, and ironed for the event. But her sister let her wear her shiny, black patent-leather shoes just for the night and she is so proud of them.

Next to her is an adorable little girl, and she has a new green dress that her mother made just for the pageant. But, if you will notice, she is still wearing her old brown shoes.

Two little Black girls are off to one side because no one invites them into a group. The one in the red dress has her entire family in the audience, including grandparents, aunts, uncles, cousins, and even some neighbors. They are all excited about her being in the pageant and they whoop and holler and clap too loud after each song. She wishes that they hadn't come at all.

Standing among the boys is a girl who is taller even than most of the boys. She hates every minute of it and wishes she were shorter and could stand with the girls.

The rest of the boys won't let the little boy in the blue print shirt into their group because they think he is a sissy. He likes girls and is sometimes even found playing house with them. He has five sisters at home.

The three boys in front are inseparable. One of them has a toy snake in his pocket, and he plans to pull it out during the quiet time in the program and let it dangle on one of the girls' necks. The other boys know he is planning this and they are ripe with anticipation. The mother of that same little boy is sitting in the audience beaming, because her son never gives her an ounce of trouble. She just doesn't understand what kind of problems the teacher is talking about with this child.

All of the boys have their hair neatly combed, slicked down with Brylcreem™. Their serviceable brown oxfords have been shined up for the event.

Uncontrollable wings cover other children's faces. The audience is full of parents and grandparents trying to take pictures of those particular children whose faces are covered. Many family albums will contain pictures showing only the top of a tot's head and the toes of his shoes.

The tallest girl will cry midway through the program, because she sang at the wrong time, when no one else was singing. She will remember the moment forever.

MATERIALS

¾ yd. natural Osnaburg cloth for background
¾ yd. dark red solid for curtains and binding
⅛ yd. each of blues, browns, reds, and greens for dresses, overalls, and shirts (try a different fabric for each)
⅛ yd. each of pink, tan, and brown for faces
¼ yd. each of brown, yellow, rust, and black for hair and shoes
2 yds. Wonder-Under™
1⅜ yds. fabric for backing
Ecru thread for machine applique
Black embroidery floss
Batting

DIRECTIONS

1. Pattern pieces for applique are found on the large pull-out pattern sheet. Cut background fabric 20½″ x 40½″ from Osnaburg cloth. Use Wonder-Under™ technique for applique pieces (see pages 7–8 for instructions) and position on background fabric, noting correct sequence. The easiest way to achieve the correct placement for appliques is to study the photograph and determine which templates need to be cut for each child. Begin to position each child, starting at left side of background fabric. The first wing is 1¼″ from the side and 5″ from the top. Refer to drawing for placement sequence of each child. After all appliques are positioned correctly, you may wish to cut away darker fabrics, which fall behind light faces. Don't worry about the wings, because it is natural for them to be transparent and for the fabrics to show through them.
2. Following manufacturer's instructions, iron appliques. Machine applique with ecru thread. Embroider faces with French knots.
3. From the dark red, cut 1 piece 8½″ x 40½″ and sew to top of appliqued piece. Cut 2 pieces 4½″ x 28½″ and sew to both sides.
4. Mark red border pieces with a 1″ crosshatch design for quilting. Layer quilt with batting and backing. Quilt around the appliques on the background fabric only. Quilt border.
5. Bind with red.

PAGEANT TIME QUILT

Placement Sequence Diagram

CHRISTMAS IS A CHILD'S FACE QUILT

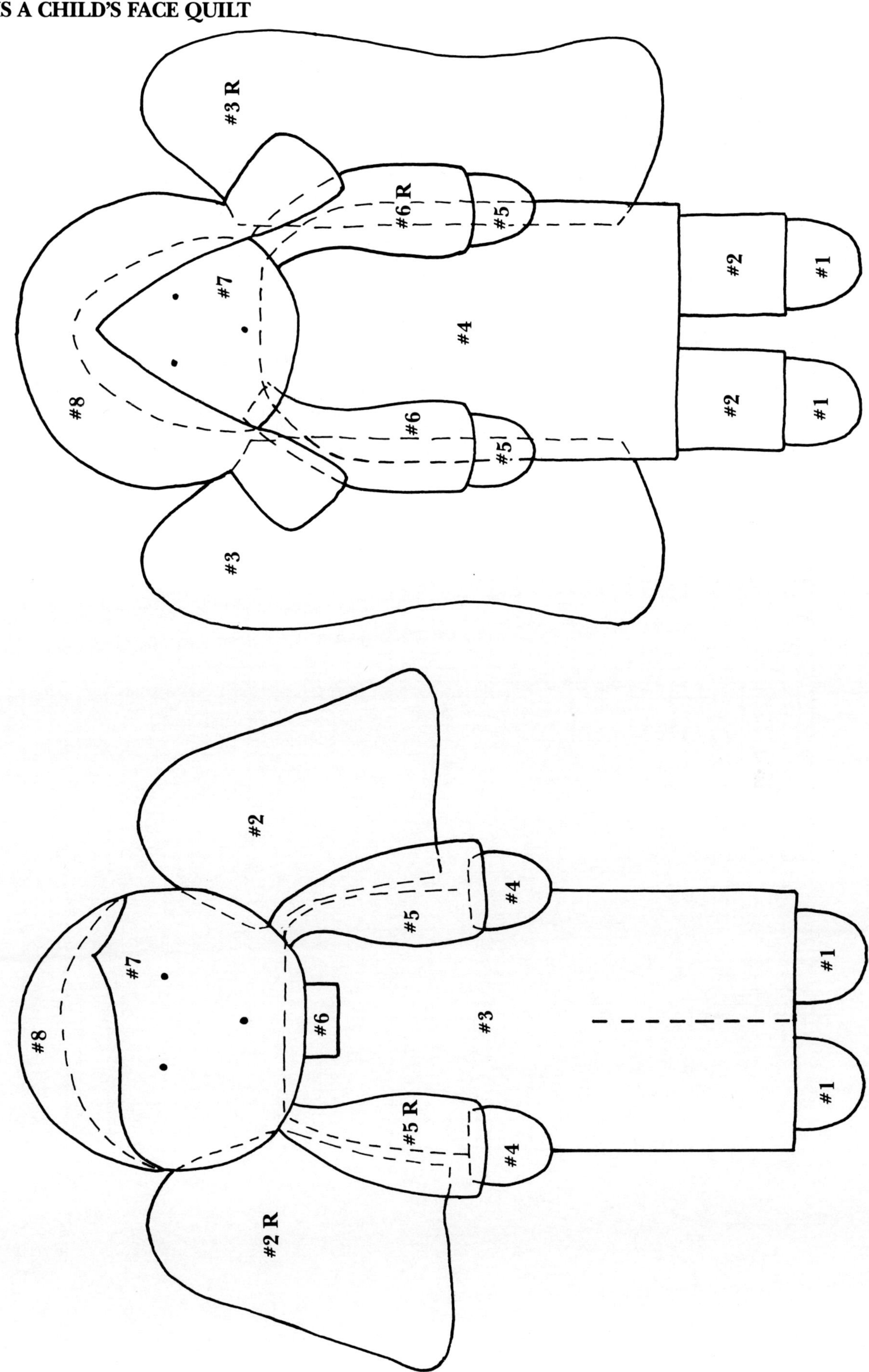

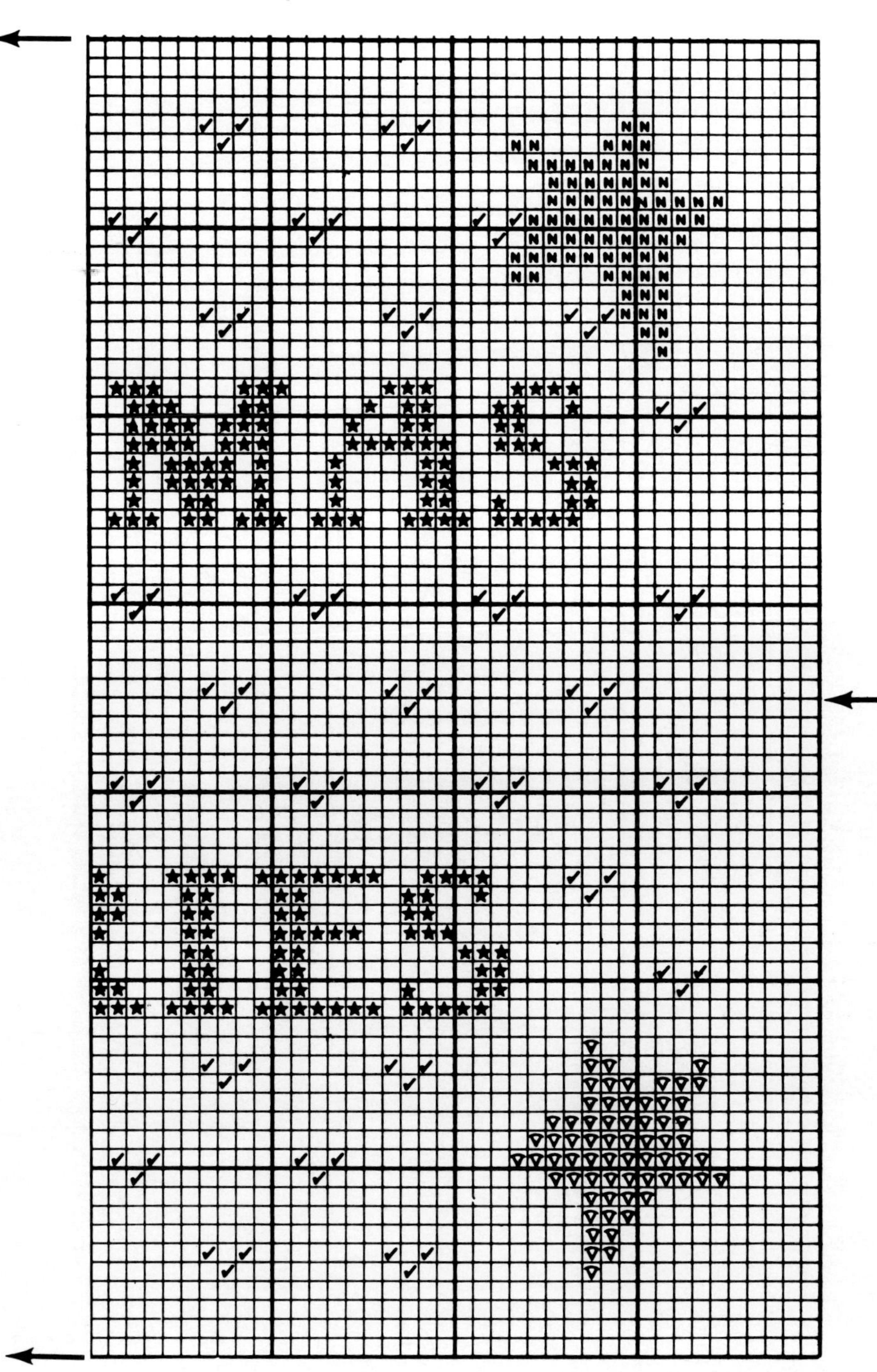

CHRISTMAS IS MEMORIES CROSS-STITCH

	DMC	COLOR
★	355	Rust
•	938	Brown
N	500	Dark green
▽	814	Maroon
#	436	Gold
✓	936	Dark blue

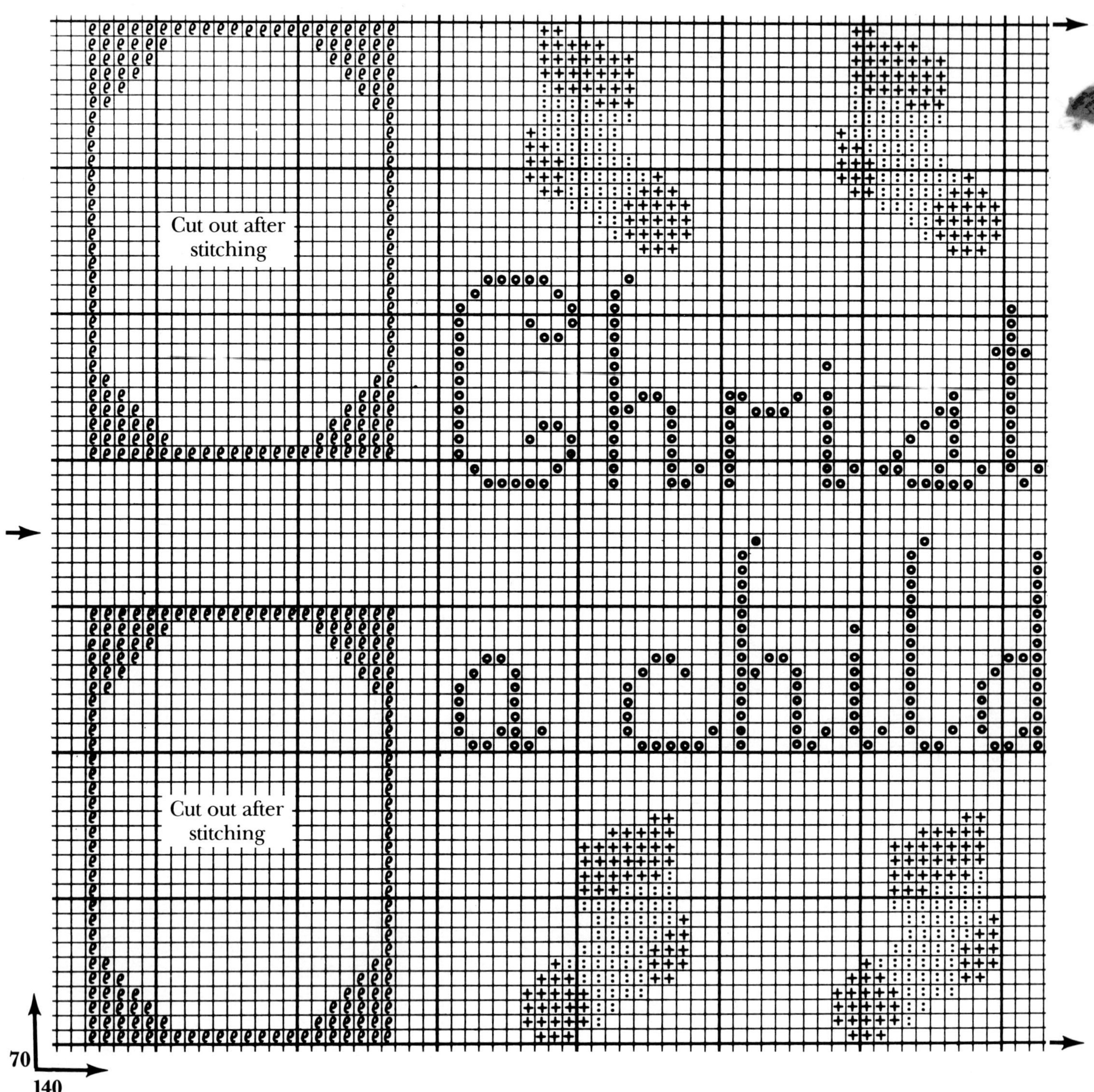

CHRISTMAS IS A CHILD'S FACE QUILT

DMC	COLOR
o 221	Dark red

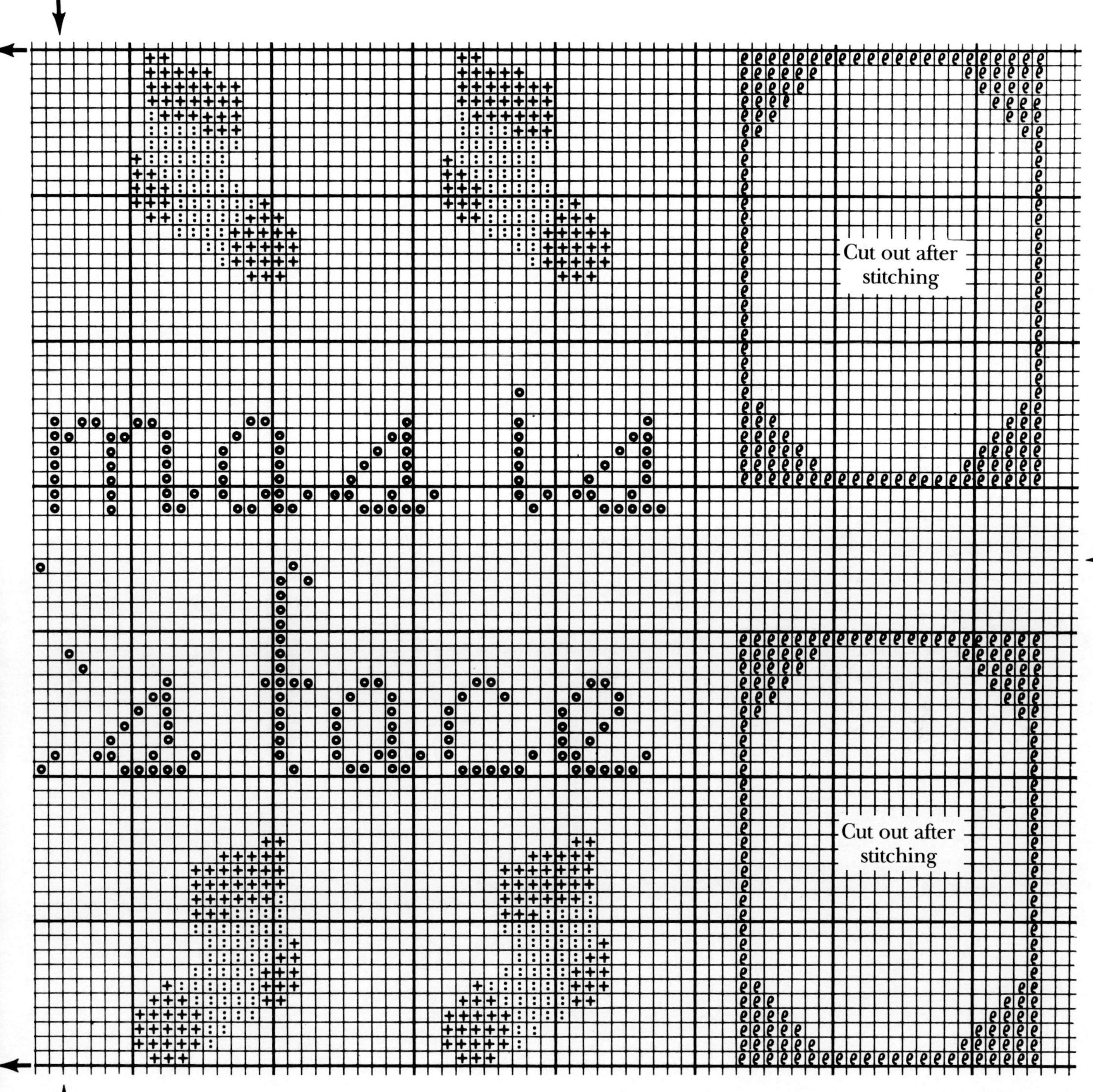

CHRISTMAS IS A CHILD'S FACE CROSS-STITCH

	DMC	COLOR
+	221	Dark red
o	501	Dark green
:		White
e		Black

LIZZIE

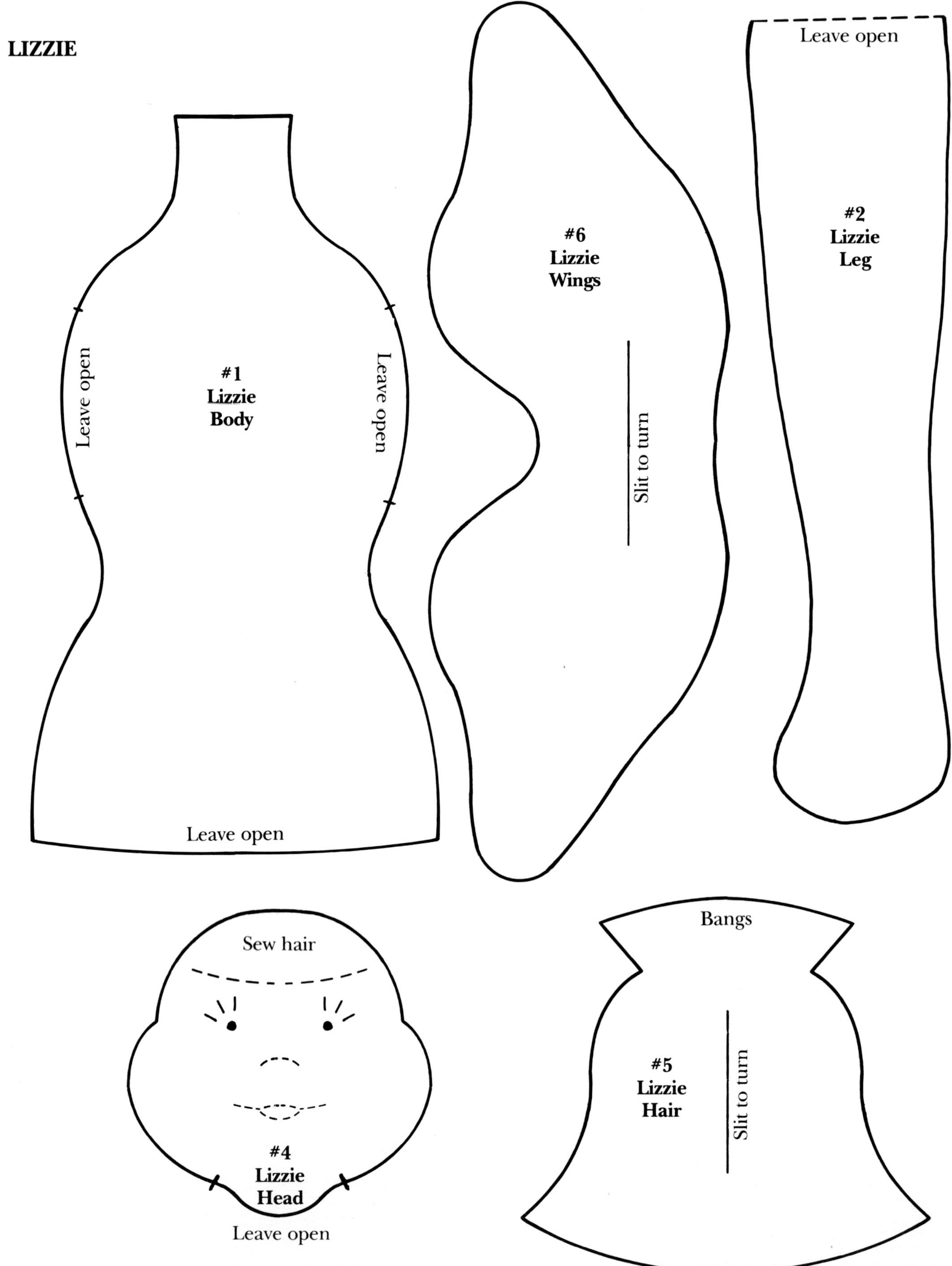
#1
Lizzie
Body
Leave open
Leave open
Leave open
#6
Lizzie
Wings
Slit to turn
Leave open
#2
Lizzie
Leg
Sew hair
#4
Lizzie
Head
Leave open
Bangs
#5
Lizzie
Hair
Slit to turn

Leave open
Shoulder
Underarm
#3
Lizzie
Arm

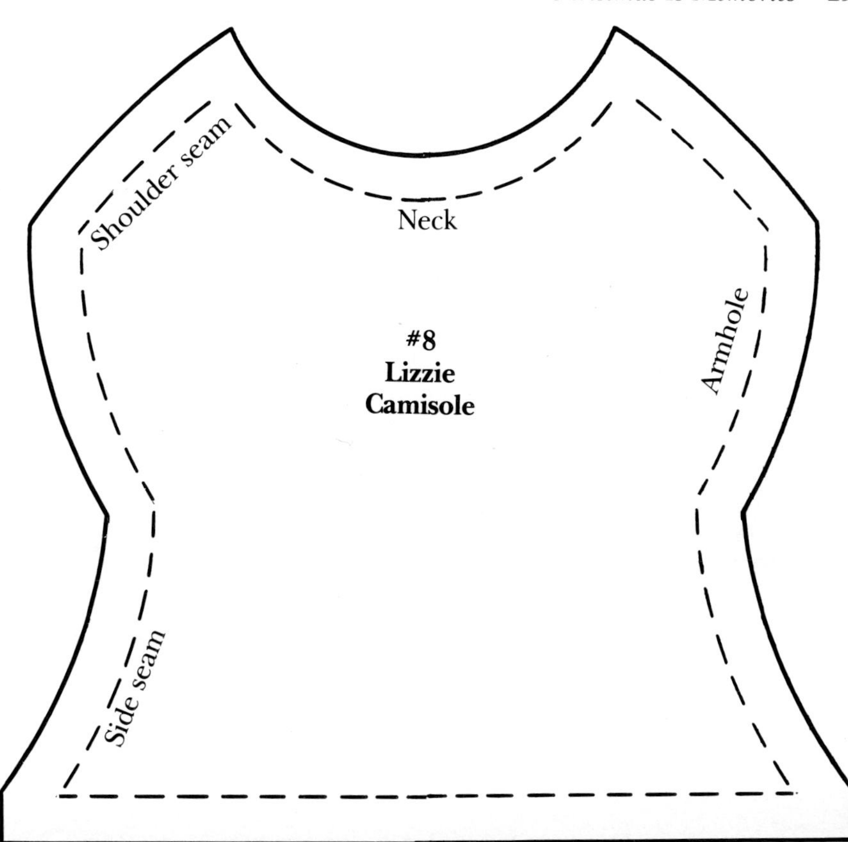
Shoulder seam
Neck
#8
Lizzie
Camisole
Armhole
Side seam

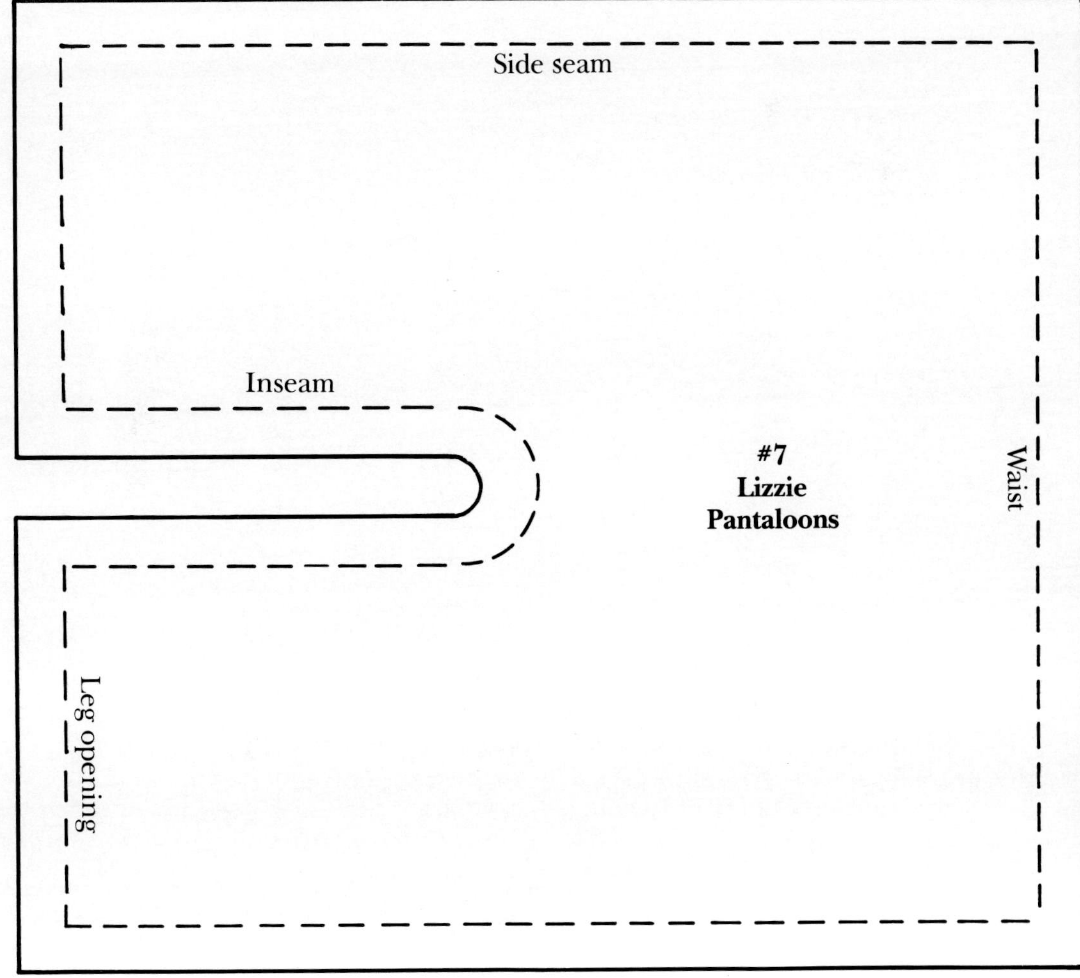
Side seam
Inseam
#7
Lizzie
Pantaloons
Waist
Leg opening

Nativity

BRENT KANE

The strength and caring of the family unit are so comforting to me and must be what causes me to relate to Nativities in any form. I have one ceramic Nativity set that I painted years ago. Each of the children in turn discovered it, and it now carries the scars of those encounters. But I just couldn't deny their desire to hold the baby carefully or touch the wise men's gifts. They were so attracted to the group and understood so easily.

BRENT KANE

BRENT KANE

The design for the brightly colored Behold Quilt (opposite page) came from a child's drawing. Fourteen Variable Star blocks surround the appliqued figures in the Silent Night Quilt (above). A simple quilt, Upon a Midnight Clear (left) depicts the spirit of Christmas.

Behold Quilt

25″ x 25″

The original drawing for this quilt was made by my step-granddaughter, Mo, who was six at the time. It was during a hectic week of baking, and the thought of one more pile of sugar on the kitchen floor was more than I felt I could handle. So out came the crayons, intended as a stocking stuffer, with a firm suggestion that she sit down and make a pretty Christmas picture. I liked it so much, I couldn't resist copying it for a quilt. I love the expressions on the faces!

MATERIALS

⅛ yd. muslin for angel and letters
⅛ yd. pink for faces, hands, and border
½ yd. black for stable, border, and binding
⅛ yd. brown for hair, hood, wood, and border
⅛ yd. purple for dress and border
¼ yd. gold for hay, star, halo, and border
⅛ yd. medium blue for baby and border
⅛ yd. dark red for blanket and border
⅛ yd. green for robe and border
⅔ yd. navy for background square
⅞ yd. fabric for backing
Black embroidery floss for faces
Batting

DIRECTIONS

1. From each of the 8 fabrics used in the border, cut a 2½″ x 12″ strip. Sew these strips together as in drawing below. Set aside.
2. Cut a 22½″ square of navy for background piece. Using patterns found on pages 34 and 35, cut out appliques.
3. Applique stable, star, and letters first. Applique remaining pieces, noting correct sequence. The overlapped areas are indicated on the pattern with dotted lines.
4. From the sewn-together border strips, cut 2″ wide strips as shown in the drawing. Sew these strips together end to end.

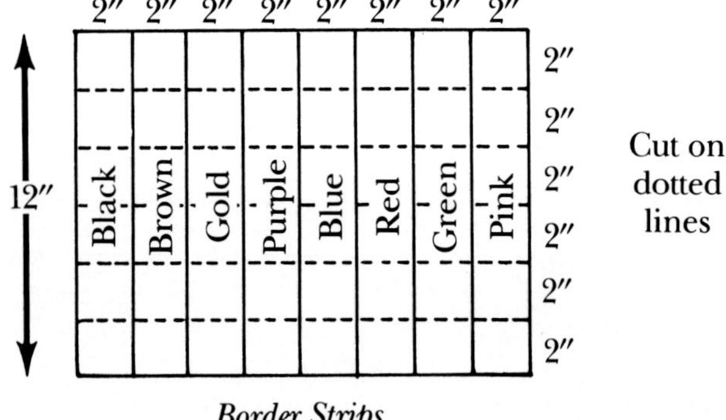

Border Strips

5. Sew pieced border to center square, removing the stitches at the end of the row to separate the strip. Trim corner pieces so they are square. Repeat for entire border. If necessary, slightly stretch border or background to make the squares come out even at the corners.
6. Layer quilt with batting and backing. Quilt around the appliques. Embroider optional faces with French knots for eyes and an outline stitch for mouth, etc. Quilt ⅛″ in from border seam.
7. Bind with black.

Upon a Midnight Clear Quilt

16″ x 11½″

MATERIALS

¼ yd. tan print for background
⅛ yd. red print for coat and border
⅛ yd. black for lamb, shoe, and border
⅛ yd. muslin for lamb and wing
⅛ yd. pink for faces, hands, and legs
⅛ yd. brown for hair, cap, pants, and cradle
⅛ yd. light blue for blanket
⅛ yd. dark blue for dress
⅜ yd. fabric for backing

DIRECTIONS

1. Cut background square 12½″ x 8″. Using pattern pieces found on page 33, cut out and position appliques onto background square; applique.
2. From red print, cut 2 strips 1″ x 8″ and 2 strips 1″ x 13½″. Sew shorter strips to sides of background piece. Sew longer strips to top and bottom.
3. From black, cut 2 strips 2″ x 9″ and 2 strips 2″ x 16½″. Sew to sides and then top and bottom, as before. Press.
4. Finish quilt with a No-Bind backing (see page 8 for instructions).

Silent Night Quilt

27″ x 21″

This quilt is dedicated to my sister, Diane Carter, who was my partner when the design first came about. It was Diane who got me into designing in a roundabout fashion, after I first cut out thousands of appliques. Diane has always been good at getting me into things!

MATERIALS

⅛ yd. brown solid for beard and wood
⅛ yd. muslin for mantle
⅛ yd. pinkish tan for faces and hands
¼ yd. brown check for robe and Variable Stars
¼ yd. blue print on light background for dress and Variable Stars
¼ yd. camel solid for hood and Variable Stars
¼ yd. tan print for blanket and Variable Stars
¼ yd. light tan print for Variable Stars
¼ yd. dark tan print for Variable Stars
¼ yd. very light tan-and-white check or print for Variable Stars
½ yd. dark blue print for background, border, and binding
⅔ yd. fabric for backing
Ecru embroidery floss for tying quilt
Batting

DIRECTIONS

1. Cut background piece 12¾″ x 19″. Cut out applique pieces, found on pages 30 and 31, and position on background. Baste or pin to hold. Applique, noting correct sequence.
2. Cut out fabrics for Variable Star blocks. Piece 14 Variable Star blocks, as shown on page 32, and press.
3. From blue background fabric, cut 8 strips 1¼″ x 5″ and 6 strips 2¼″ x 5″ for lattices to be used in the border.
4. Sew strips to Variable Star blocks as shown in piecing diagram. Sew borders to appliqued center.
5. Layer quilt with batting and backing; baste. Quilt around the outline of the appliques. With ecru floss, tie the pieced blocks and the blue border strips.
6. Bind with blue bias strips of fabric.

Piecing Diagram

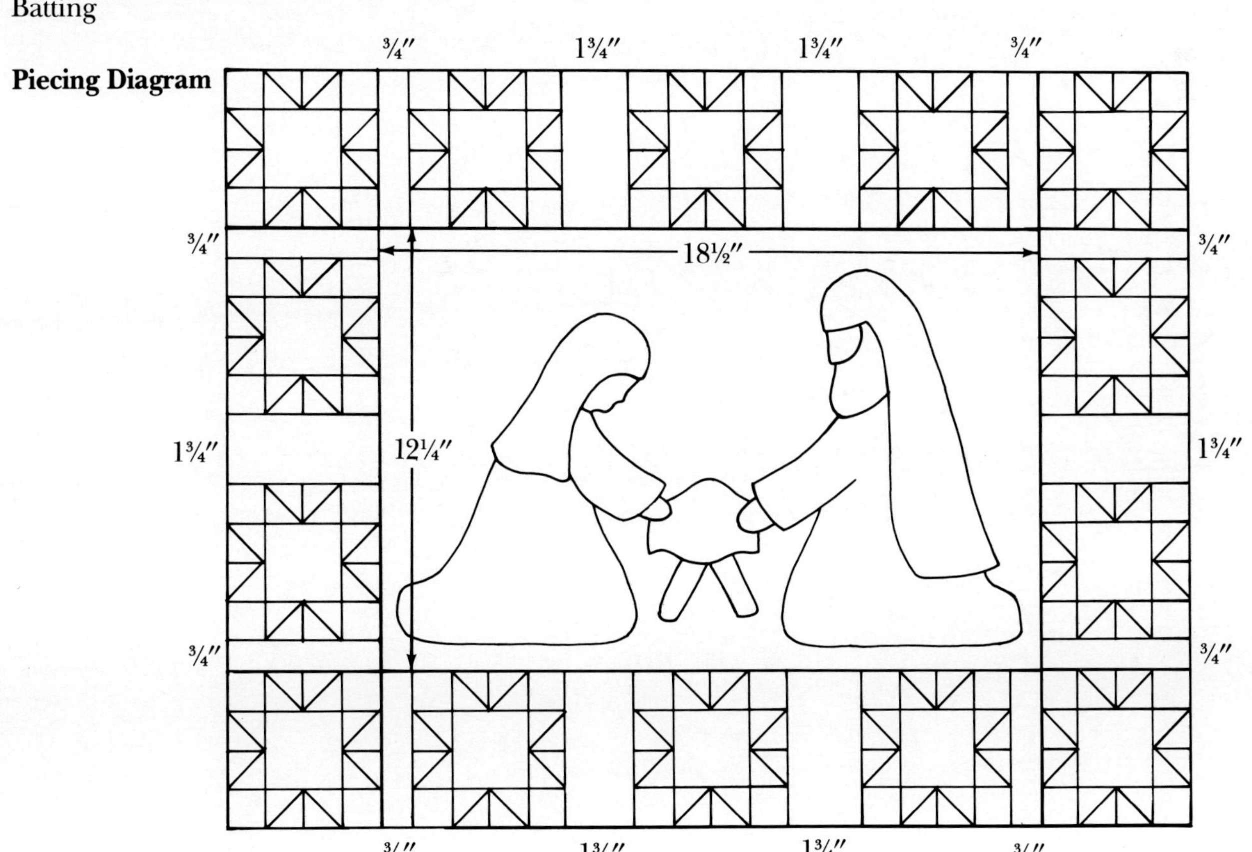

SILENT NIGHT QUILT

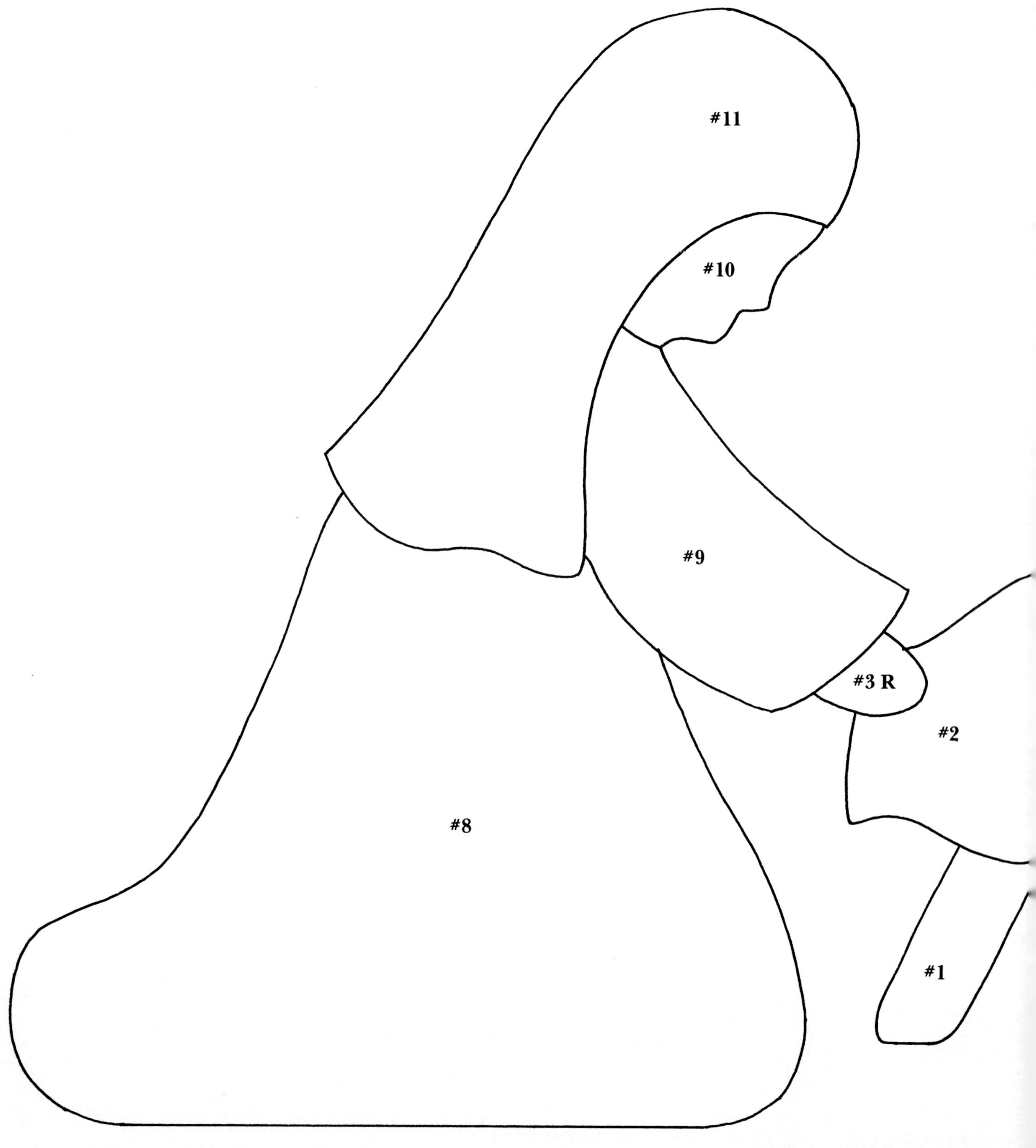

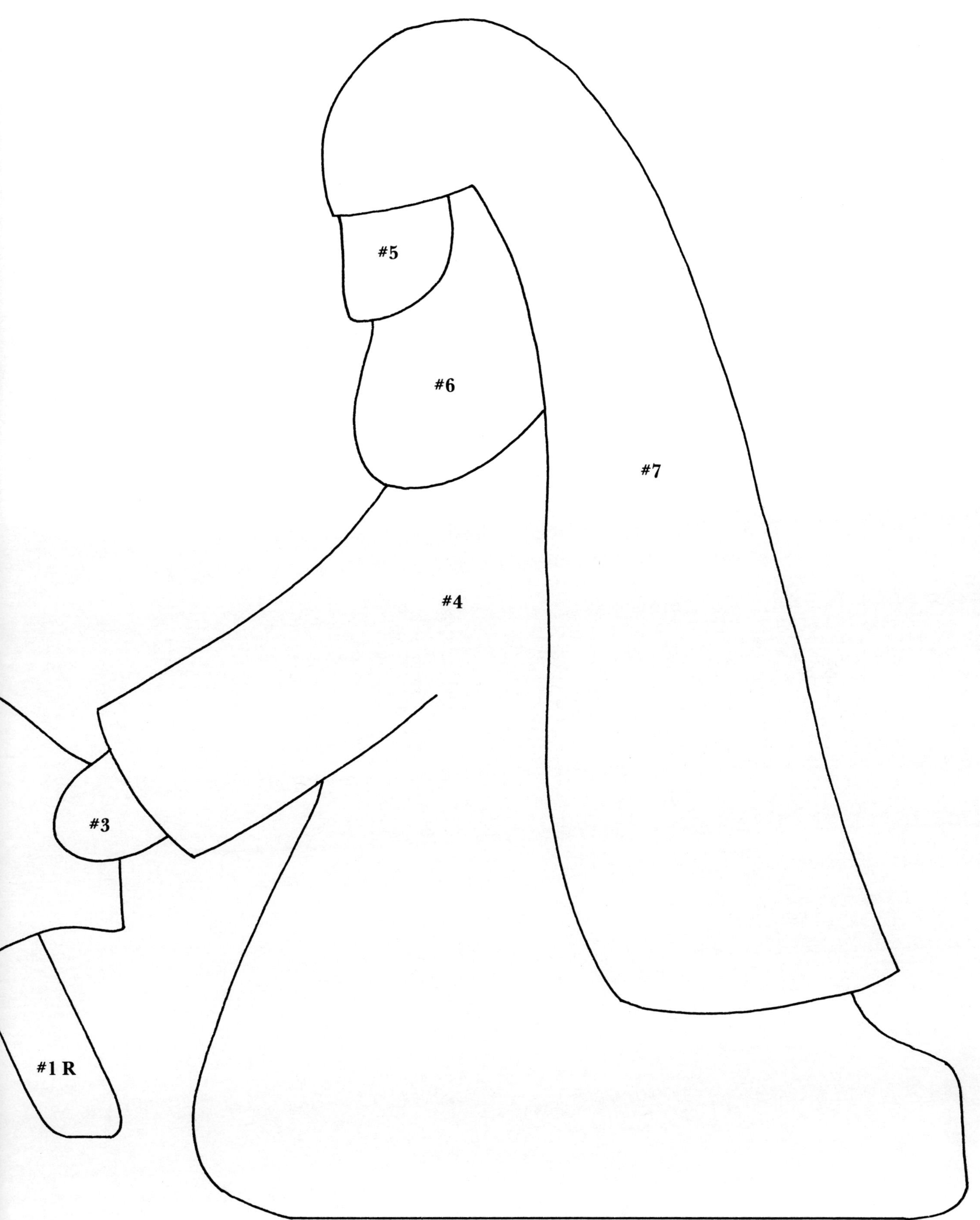
#5
#6
#7
#4
#3
#1 R

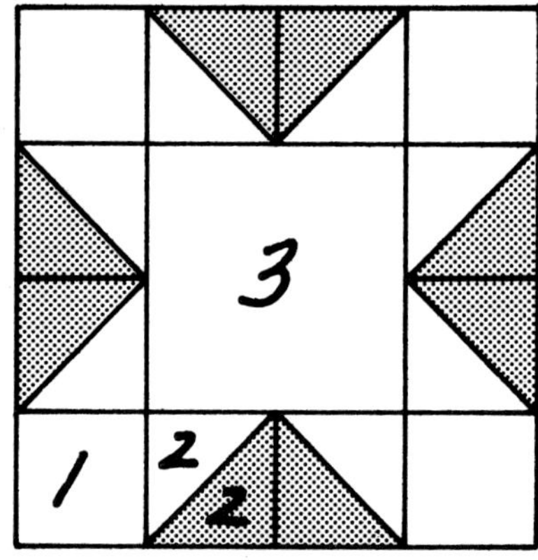

Variable Star, 4½″

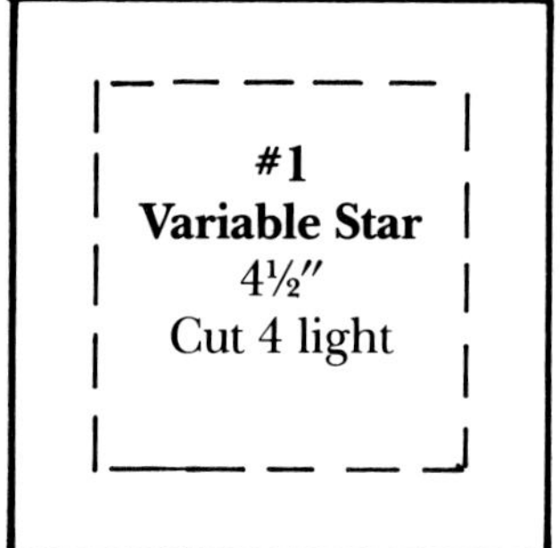

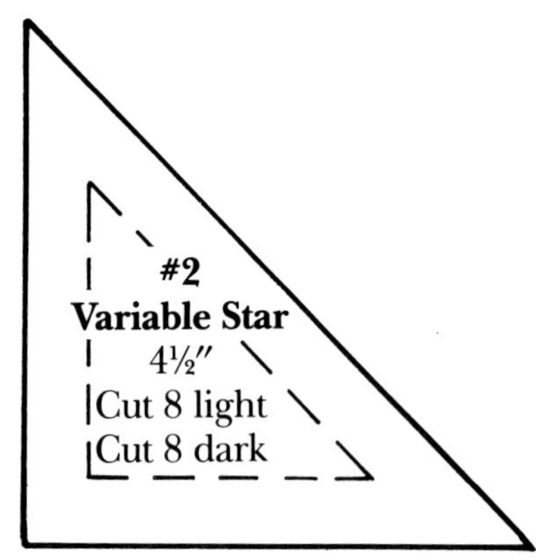

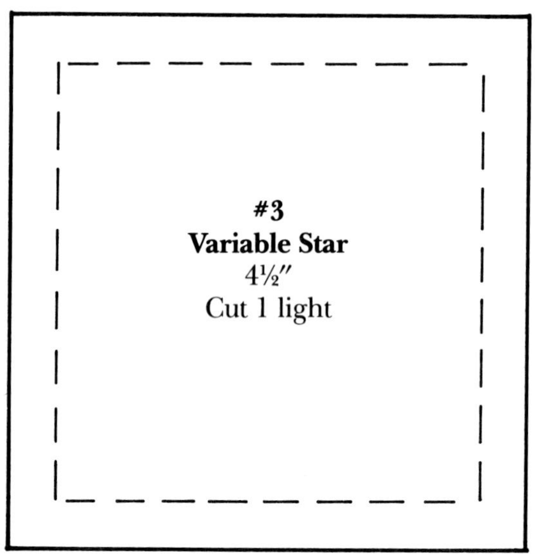

UPON A MIDNIGHT CLEAR QUILT

BEHOLD QUILT

#3
#3
#3
#3
#3
#3

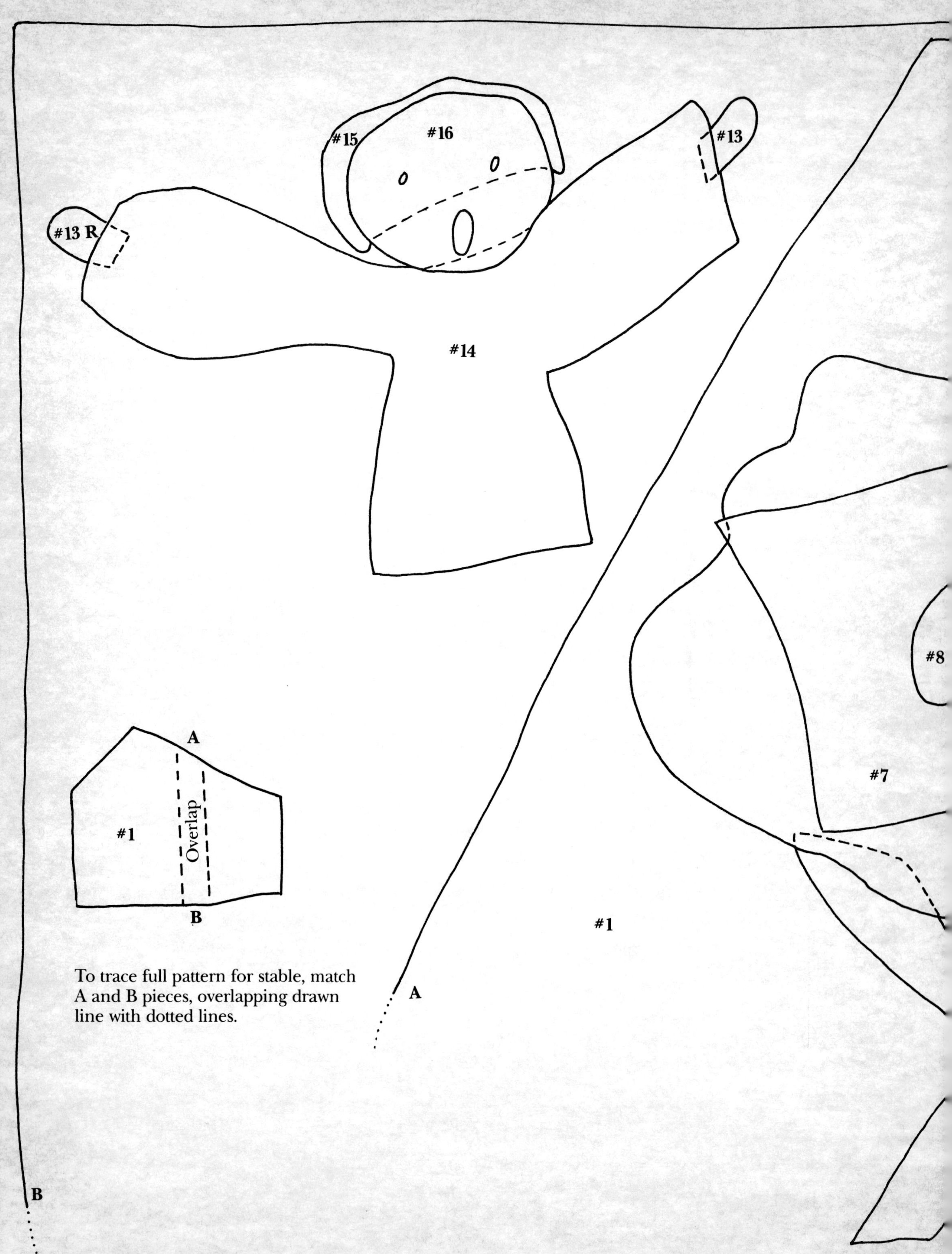

To trace full pattern for stable, match A and B pieces, overlapping drawn line with dotted lines.

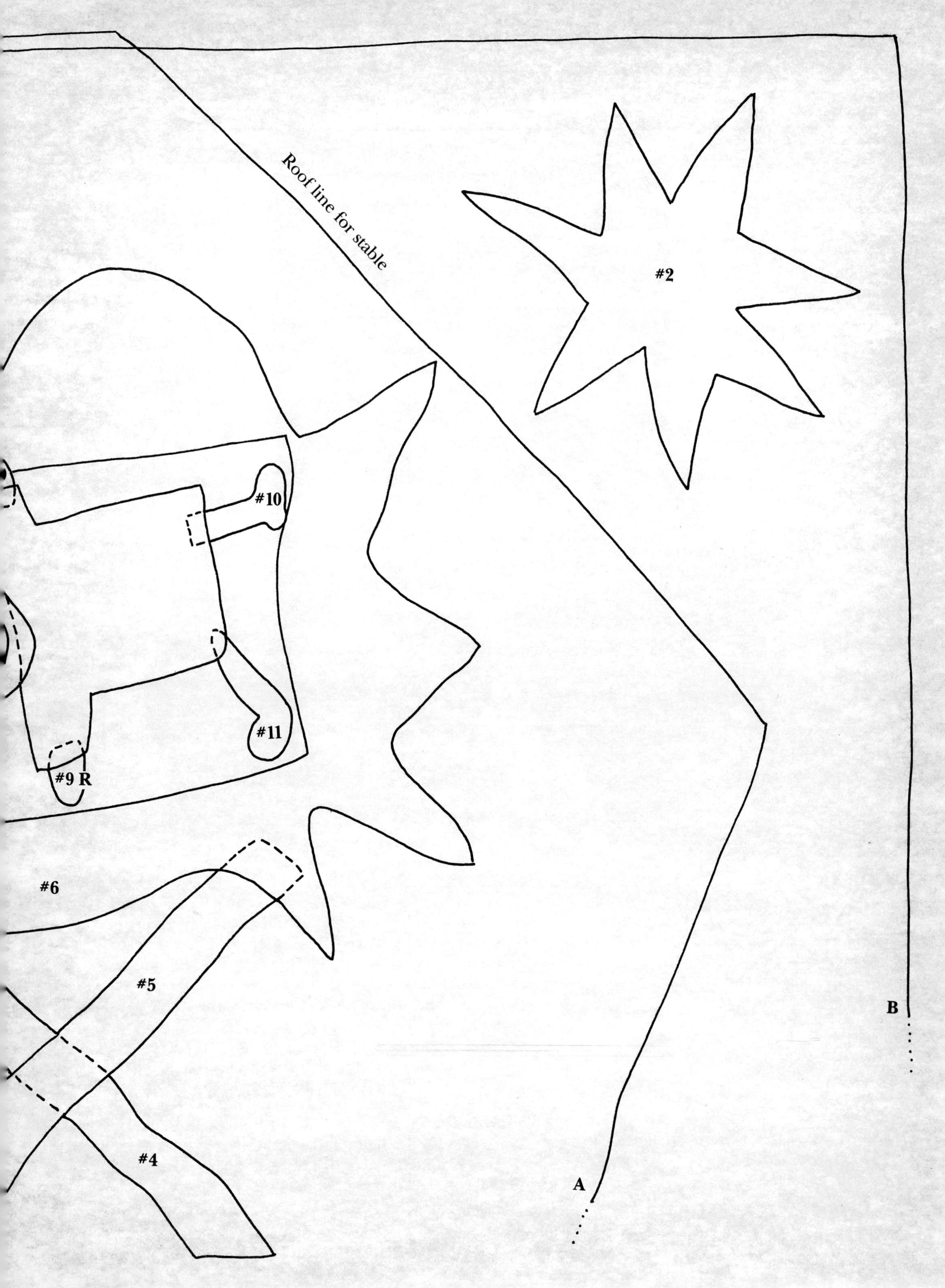
Roof line for stable
#2
#10
#11
#9 R
#6
#5
#4
A
B

Angels around the World

CARL MURRAY

Angels around the World makes a colorful quilt. The stuffed Angels around the World can be made in three sizes, while the Painted Angels around the World are 5″ tall.

The Angels around the World were inspired by the Santaberries I designed for *Santaberry Sauce.* The triangular shape worked well, but I decided I wanted them to be able to stand. So many Christmas decorations end up lying in baskets because they can't stand on their own. It was a simple matter for their wings to become their support.

When Pam Fowler saw the grouping of 5″ tall Angels around the World, she asked if she could try them as a quilt. The result of that attempt is on page 38. They are so much fun to play with, and you can use the same idea for a smaller quilt with the pattern for the 2″ Angels around the World. They could also be a simple stencil pattern, or try appliqueing them along the edge of a collar.

Angels around the World Quilt

27½″ x 37″

This quilt is perfect for using up scraps. Give yourself a challenge and make no two alike. You could even let the children pick out fabrics.

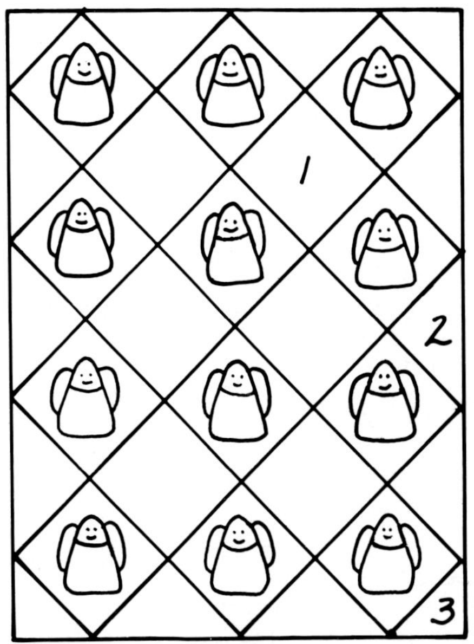

Piecing Diagram

MATERIALS

⅝ yd. tan solid for background
⅝ yd. green plaid for background
⅛ yd. each of 12 light prints for wings
⅛ yd. each of 6 green prints for bodies
⅛ yd. each of 6 red prints for bodies
⅛ yd. each of brown, tan, pink, and black for faces
1 yd. Wonder-Under™
⅞ yd. fabric for backing
¼ yd. red dot for binding
Green, pink, black, red, and white embroidery floss
Batting

DIRECTIONS

1. Cut out 12 background squares from tan, using Template #1. From green plaid, cut 6 background squares with Template #1, 10 with Template #2, and 4 with Template #3. Templates are found on pages 41 and 42.
2. Using pattern pieces for applique found on page 41 and Wonder-Under™ technique for applique pieces (see pages 7–8 for instructions), position on background squares. Following manufacturer's instructions, iron. Machine applique with matching thread.
3. Embroider faces, using a French knot for eyes and an outline stitch for mouth.
4. Following piecing diagram, assemble quilt top.
5. Layer quilt with batting and backing. Tie quilt in center of green squares and at junction of squares.
6. Bind with red.

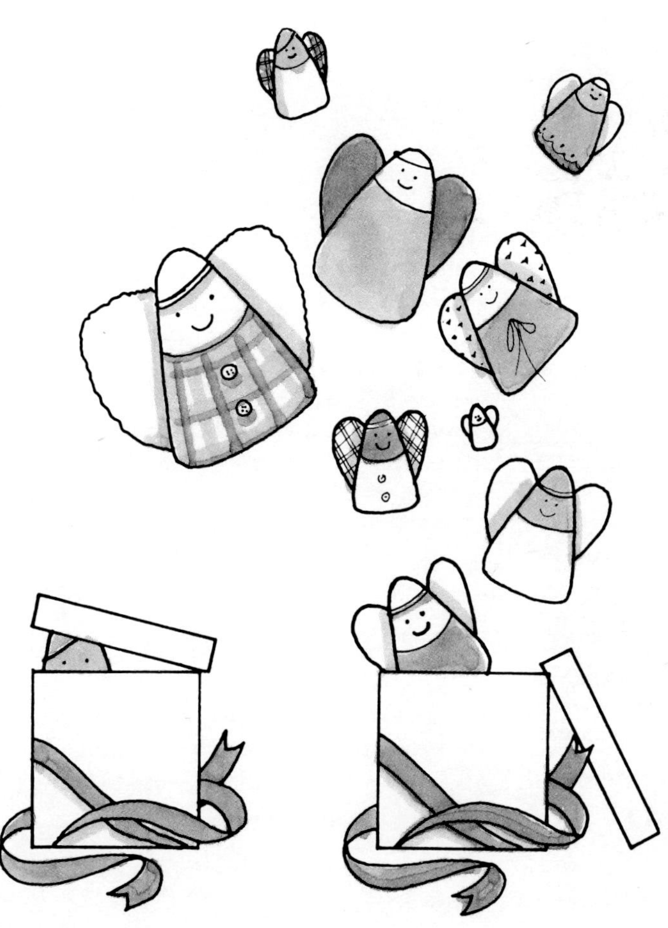

Stuffed Angels around the World

2″, 5″, and 12″ tall

I purposely did not designate any particular fabrics. I think that these shapes are so universal that anything could be used. I have used old quilt pieces, old jeans (wonderful), old flannel shirts, Sherpa, and all kinds of cotton prints for the bodies and wings. The faces, of course, can and should be any color desired.

MATERIALS

Note: Fabric requirements outside parentheses are for small angels; yardage inside parentheses is for medium and large angels.

⅛ yd. (¼ yd., ⅓ yd.) fabric for body
⅛ yd. (¼ yd., ⅜ yd.) fabric for wings
⅛ yd. (⅛ yd., ¼ yd.) fabric for faces
Embroidery floss for faces and bodies
White pipe cleaners
Polyester stuffing

DIRECTIONS

1. Pattern pieces are found on large pull-out pattern sheet. Assemble body and wings, using trace, stitch, and cut technique (see page 9); stuff.
2. Trace face piece onto folded fabric and sew. Cut out, turn, and pull over top of head snugly. Pin to hold in place. Turn under lower edge ¼″ and, using a buttonhole stitch, stitch to body with embroidery floss as in drawing.
3. Sew face with embroidery floss, using French knots for eyes and an outline stitch for mouth. Cut a pipe cleaner 2″ (3½″, 7½″) long for halo. Overlap the ends slightly and twist together. Place on head and tack in 2 or 3 spots in front and back.
4. Tie both sides of wings with 6 strands of embroidery floss. Place wings behind body with both standing up. They should be level with each other so that they will stand alone. Tie the wings to the body with floss, pulling floss up tight before tying a square knot.

Note: The large Angel has button eyes tied with embroidery floss. The body and wings are tied together through the buttons down the center. This procedure requires a long, doll-making needle.

Painted Angels around the World

5″ tall

MATERIALS

¼ yd. natural colored denim or twill
Paint of various colors
Paint brushes
Textile medium
Polyester stuffing

DIRECTIONS

1. Trace the pattern for the applique Angels around the World, found on page 41, as 1 piece, so that the outline includes the body and wings. Sew, using trace, stitch, and cut technique; turn. Lightly draw around face, body, and wings on front and back to define them. Stuff and slip-stitch closed.
2. Paint face, dress, and wings, allowing each to dry before painting the next section. If this coat is applied heavily enough, you won't need to paint a second coat. After the 3 sections are dry, you can apply the detail simply with dots or lines. You can draw on the face with a Pilot SC-UF™ pen.

PAINTED ANGELS AROUND THE WORLD AND ANGELS AROUND THE WORLD QUILT

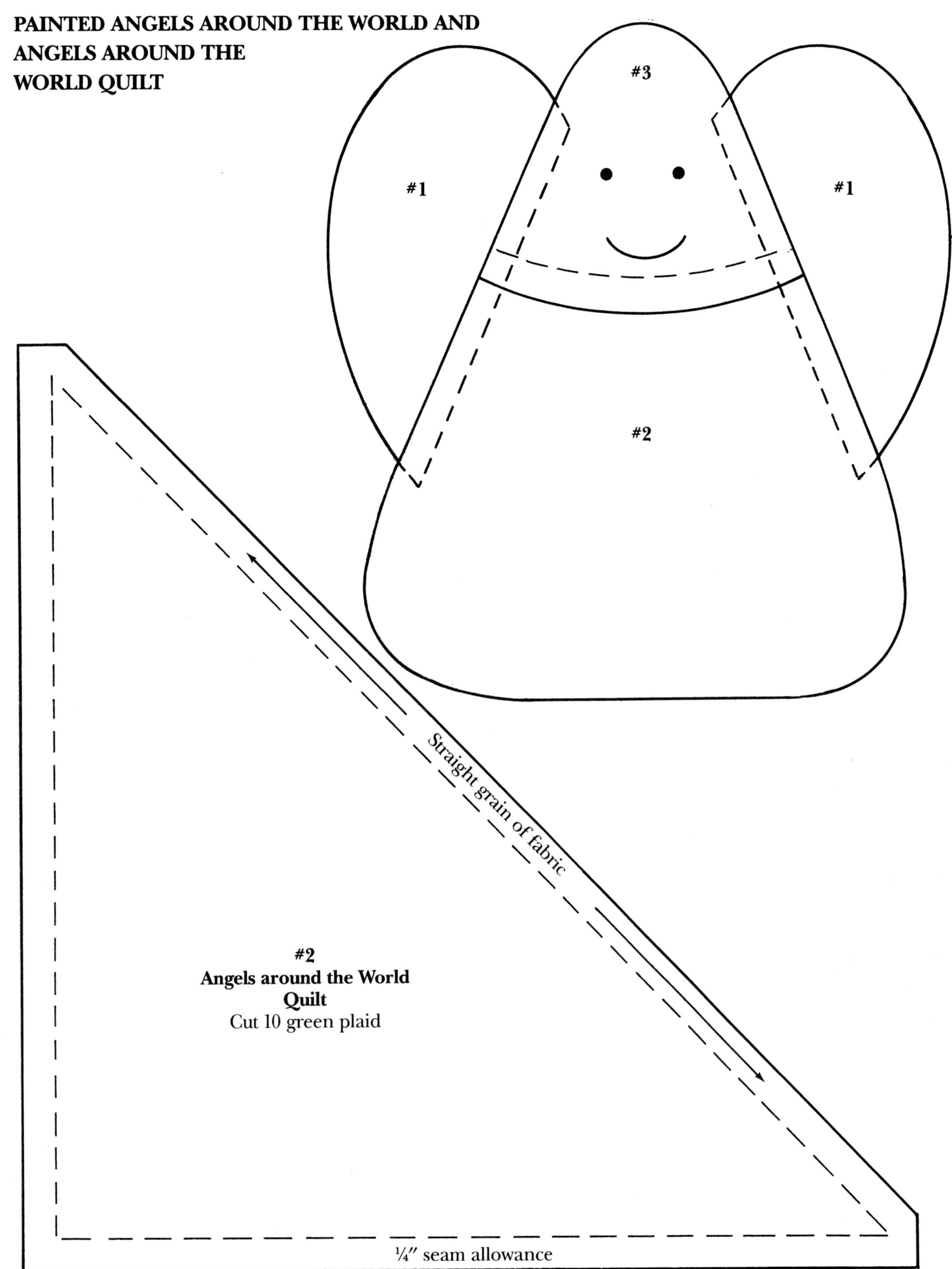

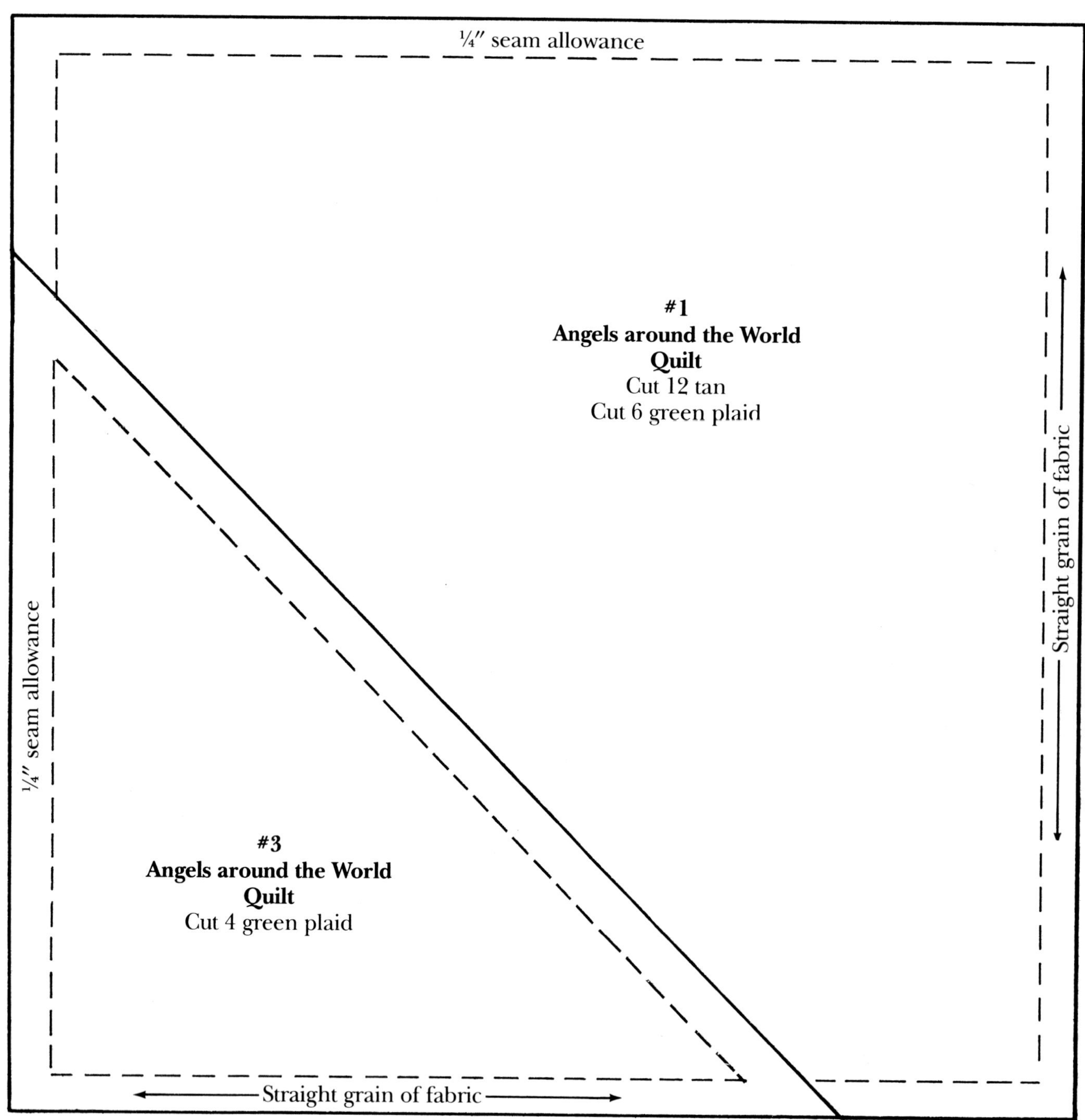
¼″ seam allowance
#1
Angels around the World
Quilt
Cut 12 tan
Cut 6 green plaid
Straight grain of fabric
¼″ seam allowance
#3
Angels around the World
Quilt
Cut 4 green plaid
Straight grain of fabric

Heavenly Angels

CARL MURRAY

In my Sunday School class, when I was very small, we had what I considered to be a magic board. It was really just a felt board, but I didn't understand how those figures stayed on. One morning, due to a delay, I was allowed to stay in the classroom and play with the felt board all by myself. I used the cut-out shapes of people, trees, and all kinds of animals to make a wonderful collage. When my Gramma returned to take me home, I had put angel wings on all of the people and animals. I remember her trying to explain what angels were and weren't. I don't think she got through to me, because I am still putting angel wings on everything!

Heavenly Angels are grouped on a window seat below the Paper Angel Garland decorating the windows. From left to right are the Angel Pillow, Prairie Angel, Guardian Angel Stocking, Herald Angel, and Country Angel.

Prairie Angel

11″ tall

The Prairie Angel's wings button on for the season and can come off for the rest of the year.

MATERIALS

⅜ yd. good-quality muslin
2 ecru buttons, ½″ diameter, shank type
Ecru embroidery floss
Polyester stuffing
Birdseed or beans

DIRECTIONS

1. Pattern pieces for the body are found on large pull-out pattern sheet. Assemble doll body with trace, stitch, and cut technique, leaving an opening on 1 side as indicated on pattern. Sew on the bottom circle and turn to right side. Stuff firmly to within 1″ from bottom. Fill the bottom with birdseed or beans. Slip-stitch opening closed.
2. Cut dress pattern, found on page 49, from muslin. Sew shoulder, underarm, and side seams. Turn under lower edge of dress ½″ and sew. Turn under sleeve edges ¼″ and sew with short running stitches, using 3 strands of embroidery floss. Leave a tail at beginning and end to draw up and tie in a bow.
3. Slit center back of dress 1″ at neck edge. Turn under neck edge and sew with embroidery floss, leaving a tail at each end.
4. Sew small running stitches on waistline with embroidery floss, starting and finishing in front; leave a tail at each end for tying.
5. Put dress on doll and tie sleeves, neck, and waist.
6. Sew wings as for Flat Sculpture (see page 9 for instructions). Trim batting to ⅛″, clip, and turn. Sew opening closed. Using your presser foot as a guide, machine quilt ¼″ from edge all the way around, then move inside this quilting line and quilt, using the first stitching line as your guide. Continue until wings are completely quilted. Make 2 buttonholes as indicated, either by hand or machine.
7. Sew buttons to back of doll body through dress. Check position of wings for accuracy. Button on wings.

Country Angel

12″ tall

This angel is a good project for recycling various old laces or trims. New trims can be lightly tea-dyed, if desired, to age them appropriately; just place in a cup of brewed tea for 30 minutes.

MATERIALS

¼ yd. tan solid for body
¼ yd. muslin for dress
1½ yds. cream satin ribbon, 1/16″ wide
12″ new or antique crocheted lace
Jute twine, 3-ply, for hair
Cardboard, 6″ square, for wings
Polyester stuffing

DIRECTIONS

1. Pattern pieces are found on pages 50 and 51. Assemble doll body and legs, using trace, stitch, and cut technique described on page 9; stuff. Insert legs into lower body opening and sew entire opening closed with a running stitch.
2. Cut dress pattern from muslin. Sew shoulder, underarm, and side seams. Turn under neck edge and sleeves ½″ and hem. Thread a needle with 15″ of ribbon and draw ribbon through neck hem, leaving a tail of ribbon at beginning and end.
3. Turn under lower dress edge ½″ and pin lace along this line. Sew dress hem and lace with a running stitch. Overlap lace slightly at the end and blindstitch.
4. Cut three 26″ lengths of jute. Knot together 3″ from 1 end, then braid until the braided section fits around doll's head; knot. Each knot should lay just at the neck. Cut off remaining jute 3″ below the knot. Sew braid to head along center seam. Unravel both ends.
5. When you put the dress on the doll, tie an 18″ length of ribbon at the waist; draw up and tie the ribbon at the neck.
6. Cut wings from cardboard and make 2 holes as indicated. To attach wings, thread an 18″ length of ribbon through the holes and tie in front.

Angel Pillow

10″ x 14″

MATERIALS

¼ yd. green print for background
⅓ yd. cream print for dress, border, and backing
⅛ yd. pink for border
⅛ yd. checkerboard print for wings
⅛ yd. pink print for dress
⅛ yd. light pink for faces, hands, and feet
⅛ yd. pale yellow for hair
⅛ yd. soft brown for hair
⅛ yd. burgundy for horn
⅜ yd. muslin for backing quilt square
1⅜ yds. contrasting piping (optional)
Batting
Polyester stuffing

DIRECTIONS

1. Cut background fabric 8″ x 12″. Using pattern pieces found on page 48, cut out and position appliques on fabric; applique, noting correct sequence.
2. From pink, cut 2 strips 1″ x 8″ and 2 strips 1″ x 13″ for border. Sew shorter strips to sides of quilt and longer strips to top and bottom.
3. From cream fabric, cut 2 strips 1¼″ x 9″ and 2 strips 1¼″ x 14½″ for border. Sew to quilt as before.
4. Layer with batting and muslin backing. Outline quilt around appliques and ⅛″ from border seams.
5. Stitch piping to outside edge of pillow front, if desired.
6. From cream fabric, cut a piece 10½″ x 14½″. Sew to quilt, leaving 4″ of the center lower edge open. Stuff pillow and slip-stitch opening closed.

Guardian Angel Stocking

18″ long

MATERIALS

½ yd. red solid for stocking
½ yd. light tan for lining, crib legs, and binding
Batting
⅛ yd. white for wings and blanket
⅛ yd. blue-green for robe and hood
⅛ yd. red print for dress
⅛ yd. pink for faces and hands
Ecru embroidery floss

DIRECTIONS

1. Pattern pieces are found on large pull-out pattern sheet. Cut out 2 stockings, 2 battings, and 2 lining pieces, reversing pattern as necessary.
2. Cut out appliques. Position on stocking front and applique, noting correct sequence.
3. Layer lining, batting, and appliqued front as for quilting. Pin layers together. Tie stocking through all layers with ecru floss. Repeat for stocking back.
4. With stocking fabrics together, pin front to back; sew.
5. To bind top edge, cut a 2″ x 16″ strip from tan fabric. Sew short ends together to make a circle. Fold in half lengthwise and sew to top edge of stocking, matching raw edges. Fold toward lining and blindstitch.
6. From tan fabric, cut a strip 1½″ x 8″. Fold in half lengthwise and press. Fold raw edges in toward center line and press. Sew pressed edges together close to outer edge. Bring ends together and sew to inside of stocking 1″ below top edge.

Herald Angel Doll

16″ tall

MATERIALS

½ yd. muslin for body, petticoat, and wings
⅓ yd. dark green solid for dress
⅓ yd. red and green print for jumper and cap
24″ red twisted satin cord
21″ cream satin ribbon, ¹⁄₁₆″ wide
24″ ecru gathered, crocheted lace
1 ball of light gold, heavy pearl cotton
Metallic thread for quilting wings (optional)
Batting
Polyester stuffing
Knitting needles to curl hair (must be aluminum)

DIRECTIONS FOR DOLL:

1. Pattern pieces are found on pages 52–54. Assemble body, arms, and legs with trace, stitch, and cut technique (see page 9); stuff.
2. Turn under raw edges of arm openings and baste. Insert arms, with thumbs up, and blindstitch to body. Push stuffing into joined section. Remove basting.
3. Insert legs into openings, having toes pointed out.

Turn under raw edge of lower body and sew through all layers with a running stitch.

4. Cut 4 head pieces and sew center front seams and center back seams. Sew both sections together at center side seams. Turn under raw edge and baste. Stuff head and place over neck; blindstitch to body. Remove basting.
5. To make hair, cut pearl cotton to 15″ lengths and lay across a strip of muslin 15″ x 4¼″. Mark the center of the strip by folding in half widthwise. Cover strip completely with cotton so that there is a thick uniform covering of cotton. Sew the cotton to the strip with a zigzag stitch. Cut strip close to stitching on each side; it will be about ½″ wide.

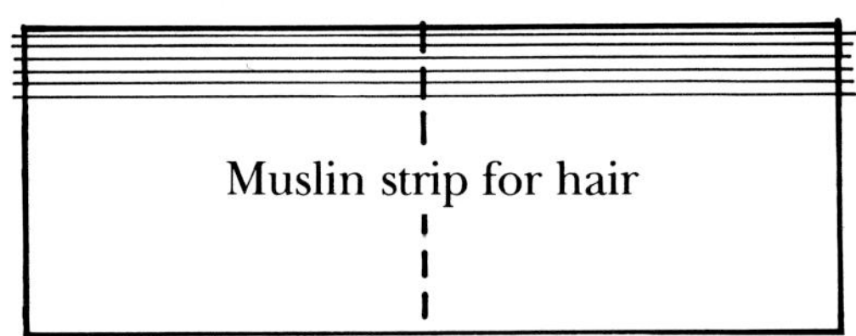

Lay on pearl cotton lengths until muslin is uniformly covered

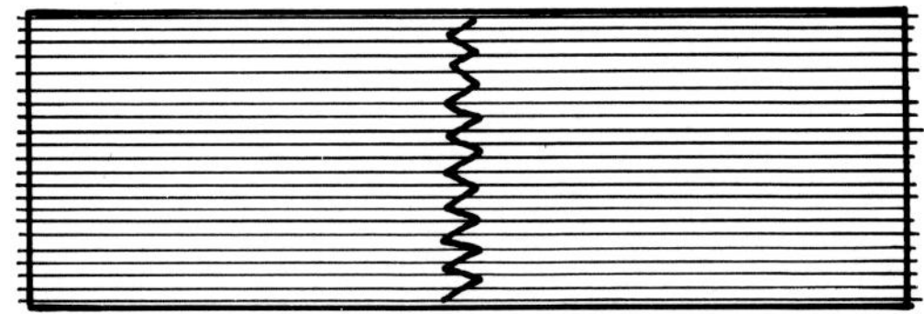

Zigzag pearl cotton onto muslin

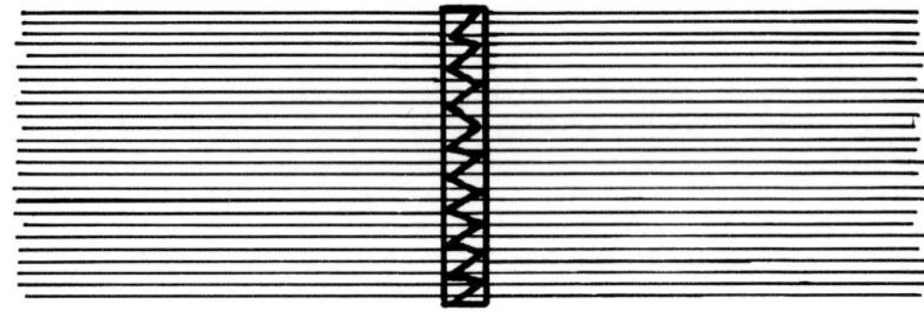

Cut muslin close to stitching

6. Wet hair completely and wind each side around knitting needles. Place on a cookie sheet in a 200-degree oven until dry. Sew hair to head along center back/front seam. Start at back of neck and sew towards front with running stitches.

DIRECTIONS FOR CLOTHES:

1. Cut a piece of muslin 10½″ x 24″ for petticoat. Sew together along short sides. Turn under lower edge ½″ and hem. Sew lace at lower edge so that it extends past the hem by ½″. Fold petticoat in quarters and press for dart lines. Make 4 darts by measuring and marking as in illustration; sew. Turn under top edge ½″ and sew, leaving room for a ribbon. Thread a large-eyed needle with 1/16″ wide ribbon and run through casing, leaving equal tails at beginning and end. After putting on doll, draw up and tie in a bow.

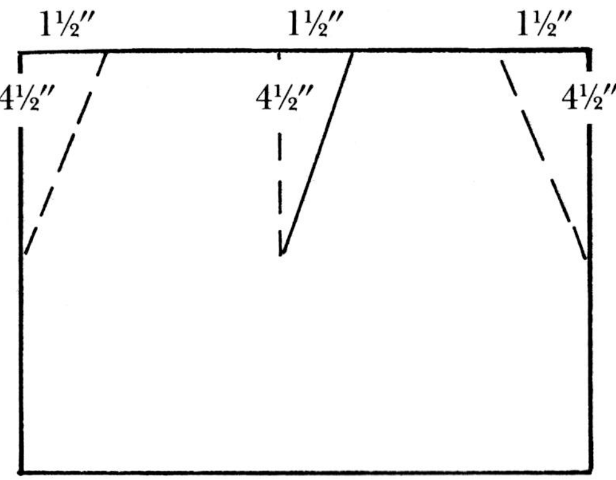

Petticoat darts (make 4)

2. Cut out 1 dress bodice front, 2 dress bodice backs, 2 sleeves, and a skirt that is 10″ x 22″. Sew bodice front to bodice backs at shoulder seams. Gather sleeves as indicated on pattern and sew to armhole edges of bodice. Turn under edge of sleeves ¼″ and hem. Sew front to back at underarm and side seams. Turn under 1 raw edge of center back bodice. If dress won't be removed, this opening can be sewn together after the dress is put on the doll. Otherwise, snaps can be sewn as back closings.
3. Sew skirt together at short sides, leaving top 2″ unsewn. Turn under lower edge 1″ and hem. Gather top edge to match lower bodice. Turn under 1 edge of unsewn top to match bodice center back opening. Sew skirt to bodice.
4. Cut out 1 jumper bodice back, 2 jumper bodice fronts, and a skirt that is 8″ x 21″. Sew fronts to backs at shoulder and side seams. Clip curves at armhole openings and hem with a running stitch. Turn under and hem front and neck edges. Turn under and hem 3 sides of skirt, slightly curving the lower front edges as you sew them. Gather the top edge to match lower edge of bodice; sew. The red cord holds the jumper closed.
5. Sew wings as for Flat Sculpture (see page 9). Lightly draw on quilting design and quilt with metallic thread. Tack wings to jumper back. Place opening seam against jumper.
6. Cut a 6″ diameter circle from jumper fabric. Turn under the outside edge ¼″ and sew. With a double, knotted thread, sew a line of running stitches ½″ in from the edge. Draw up thread to fit around doll's head. Tie off on the inside of cap. Place cap on head and distribute hair evenly, covering side seams well.

Paper Angel Garland

4″ tall x 18″ long

Just like we made as children! Hang them on your tree or on the windows.

MATERIALS

White, glossy shelf paper, wrapping paper, or lightweight tracing paper
Small, pointed paper-cutting scissors

DIRECTIONS

1. Cut paper into a strip 5″ x 18″. Trace ½ of angel pattern, found below, onto left end of paper, keeping the outside edge of the design close to the outside edge of the paper.
2. Fold paper on center line of angel and make next fold, accordion style, even with outside edge of paper. Repeat folds, until you reach end of paper. Cut off any excess at end.

3. Stapling the paper in areas that will be cut away will help to hold it while you are cutting. Cut out design. Do not cut apart at wings! Leave at least ¼″ of the paper fold uncut.
4. Open out and press flat with your fingers.

PAPER ANGEL GARLAND

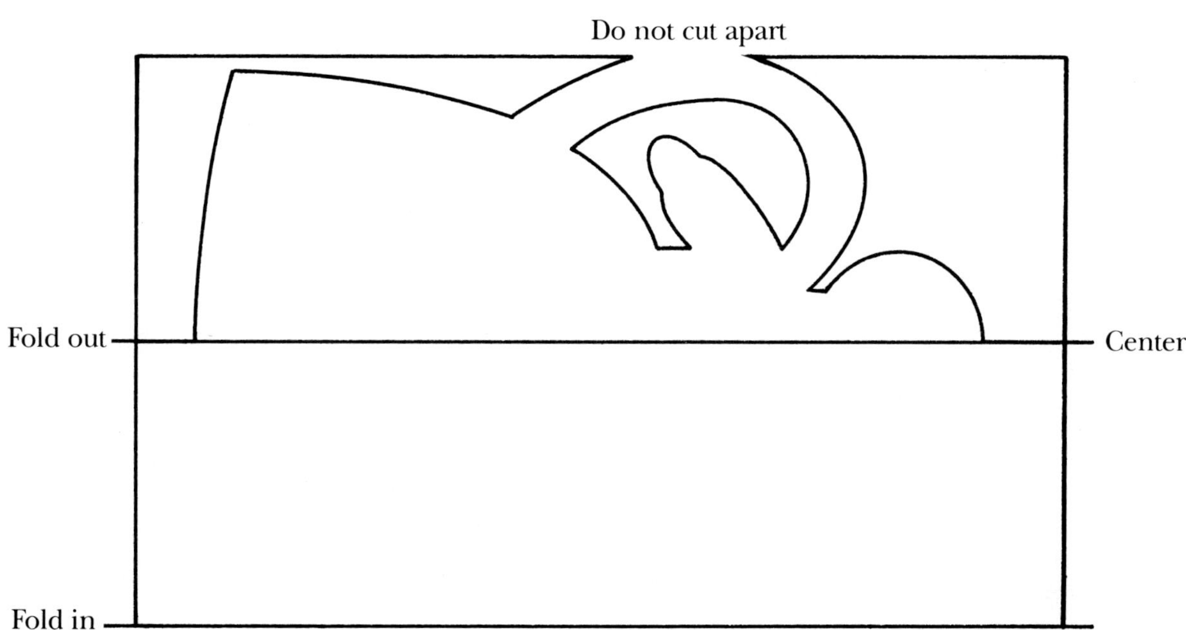

ANGEL PILLOW

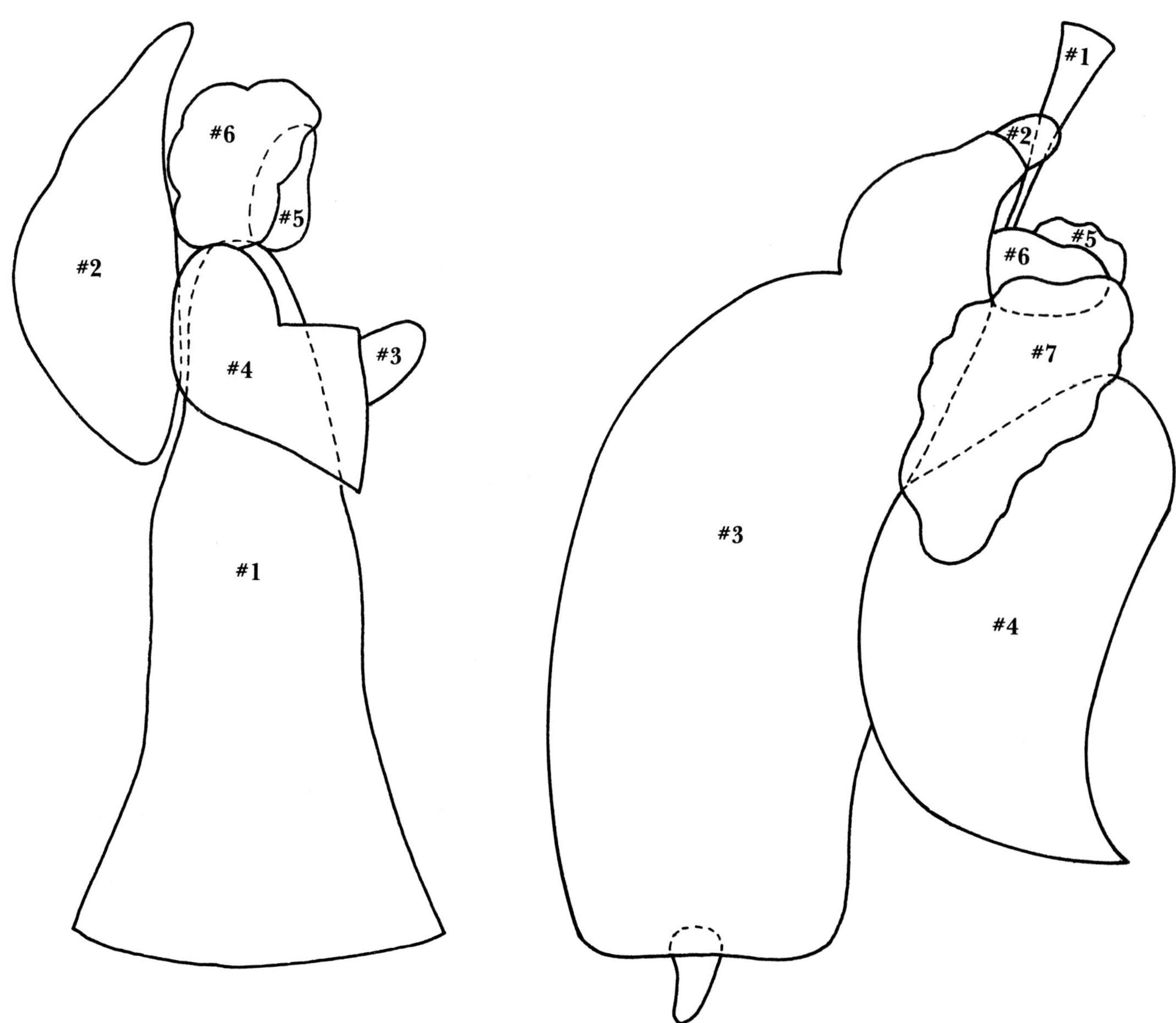

PRAIRIE ANGEL

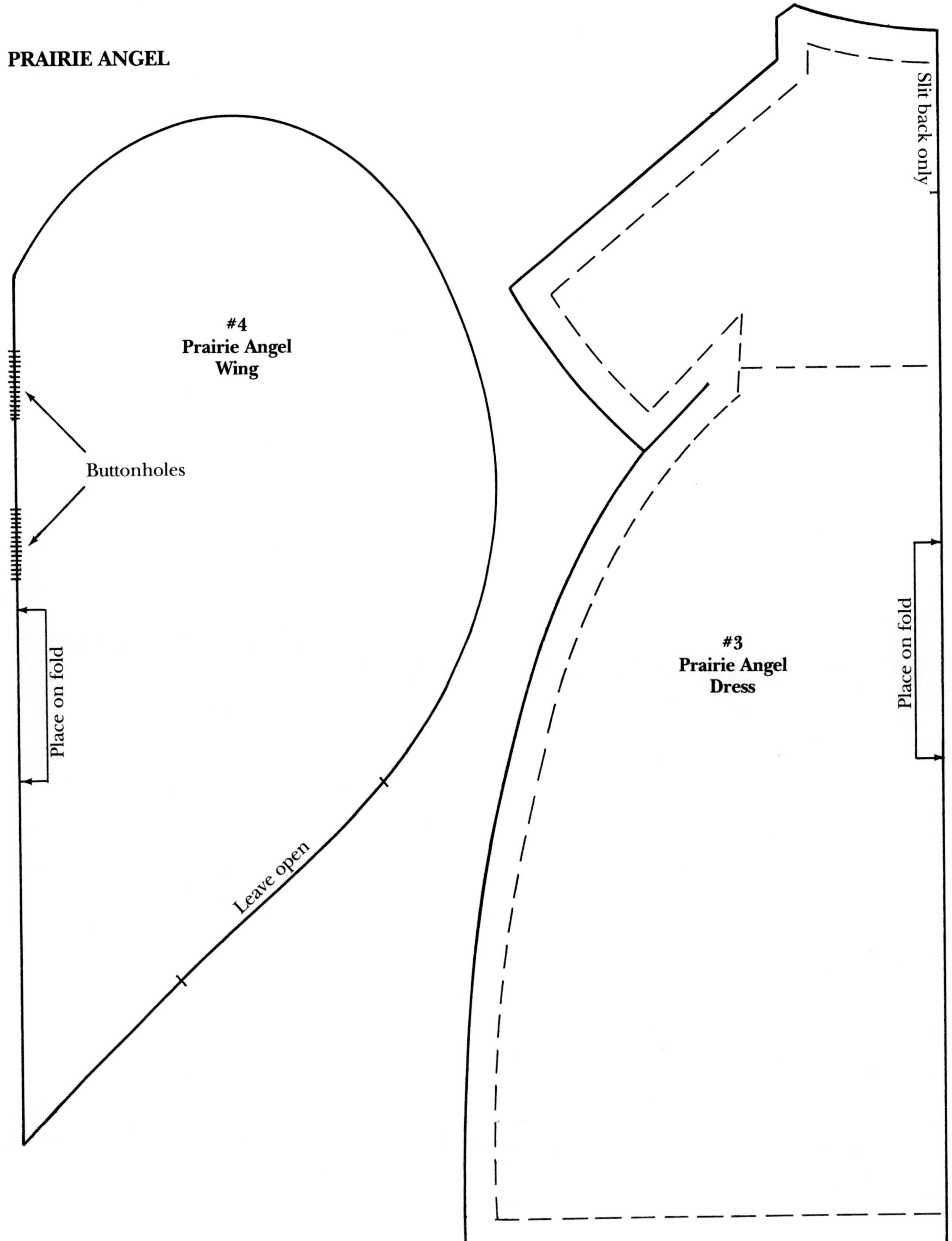

COUNTRY ANGEL

#1
Country Angel
Body
Cut 2

Leave open

Leave open

#2
Country Angel
Leg
Cut 4

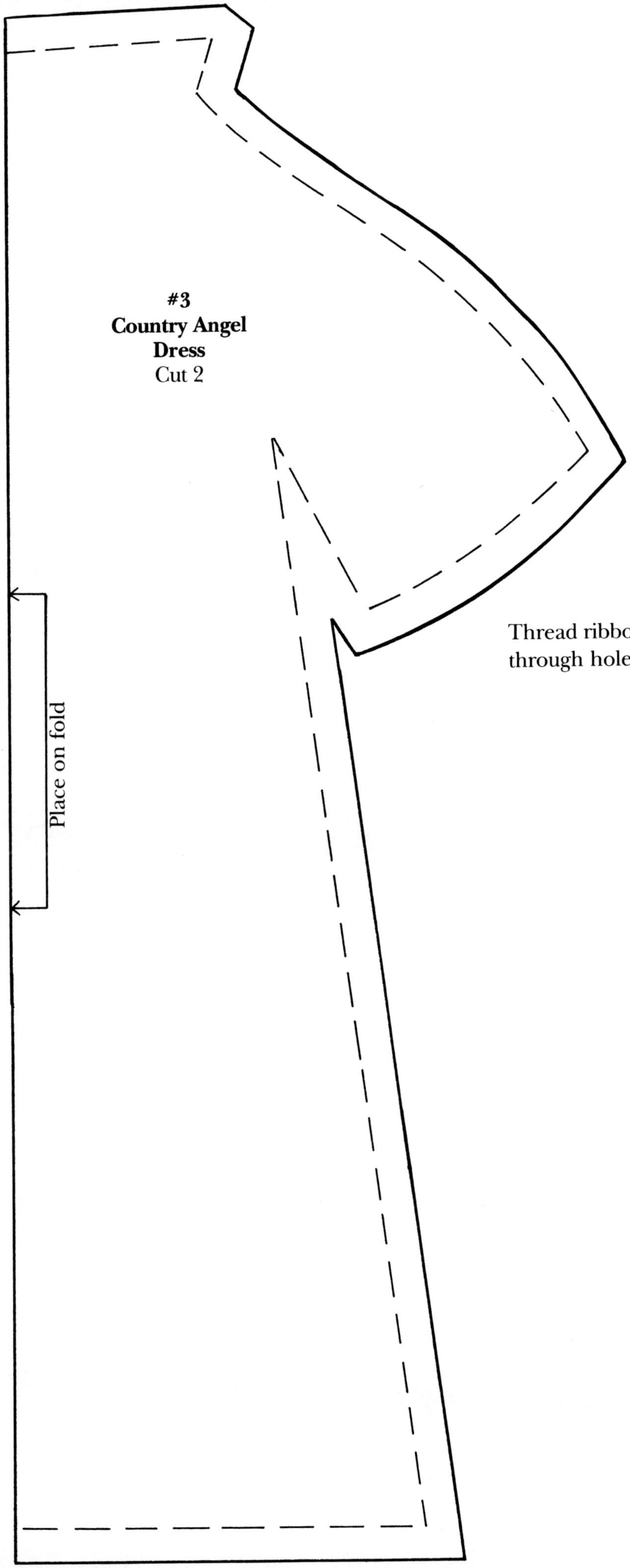

#3
Country Angel
Dress
Cut 2

Place on fold

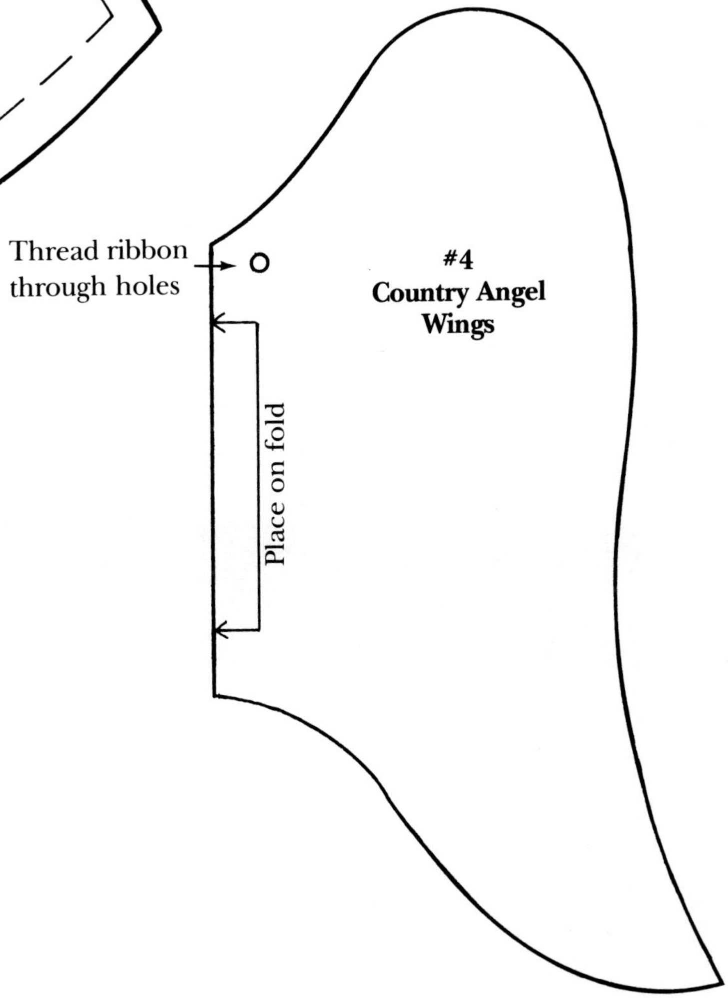

Thread ribbon through holes

#4
Country Angel
Wings

Place on fold

HERALD ANGEL

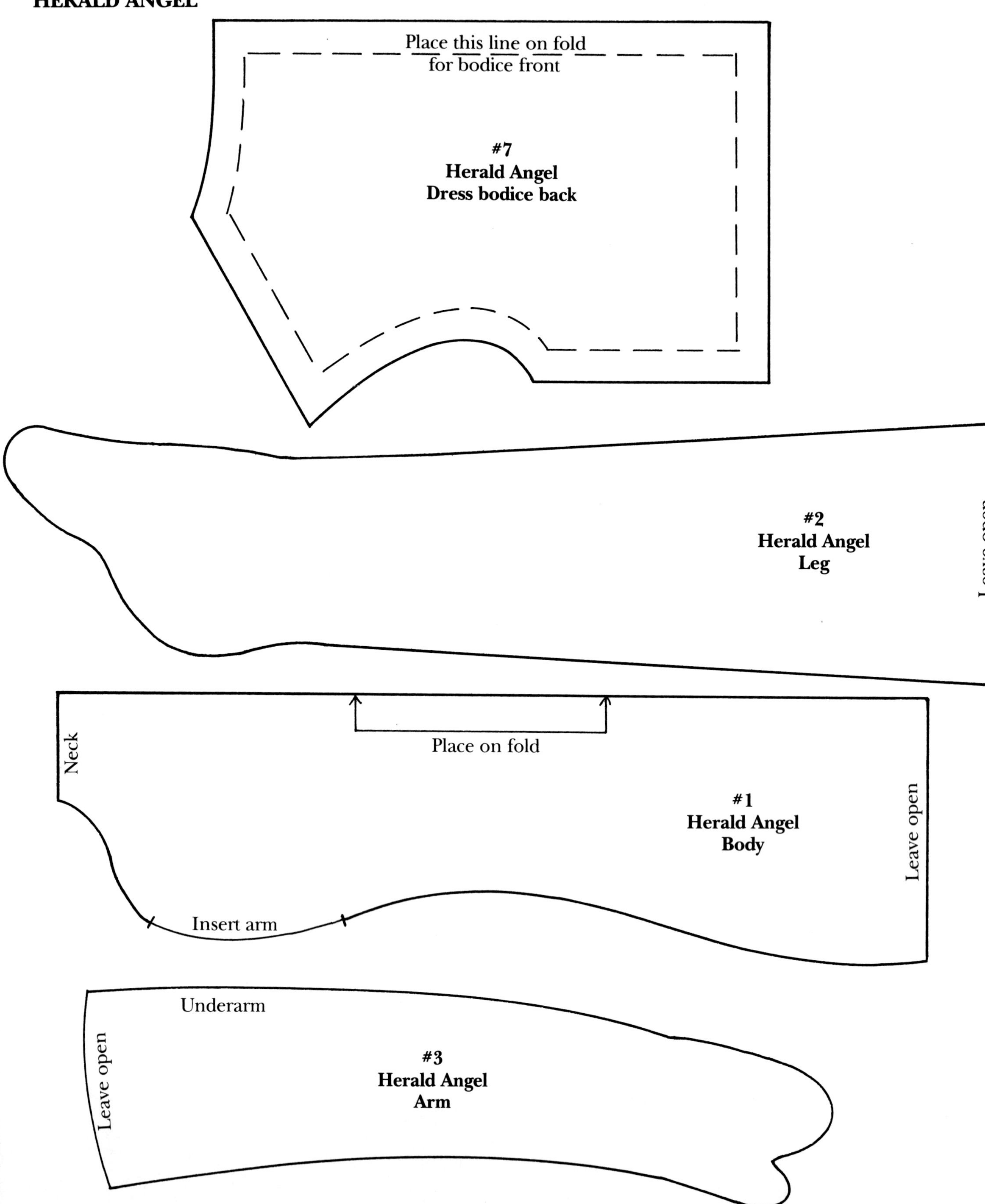

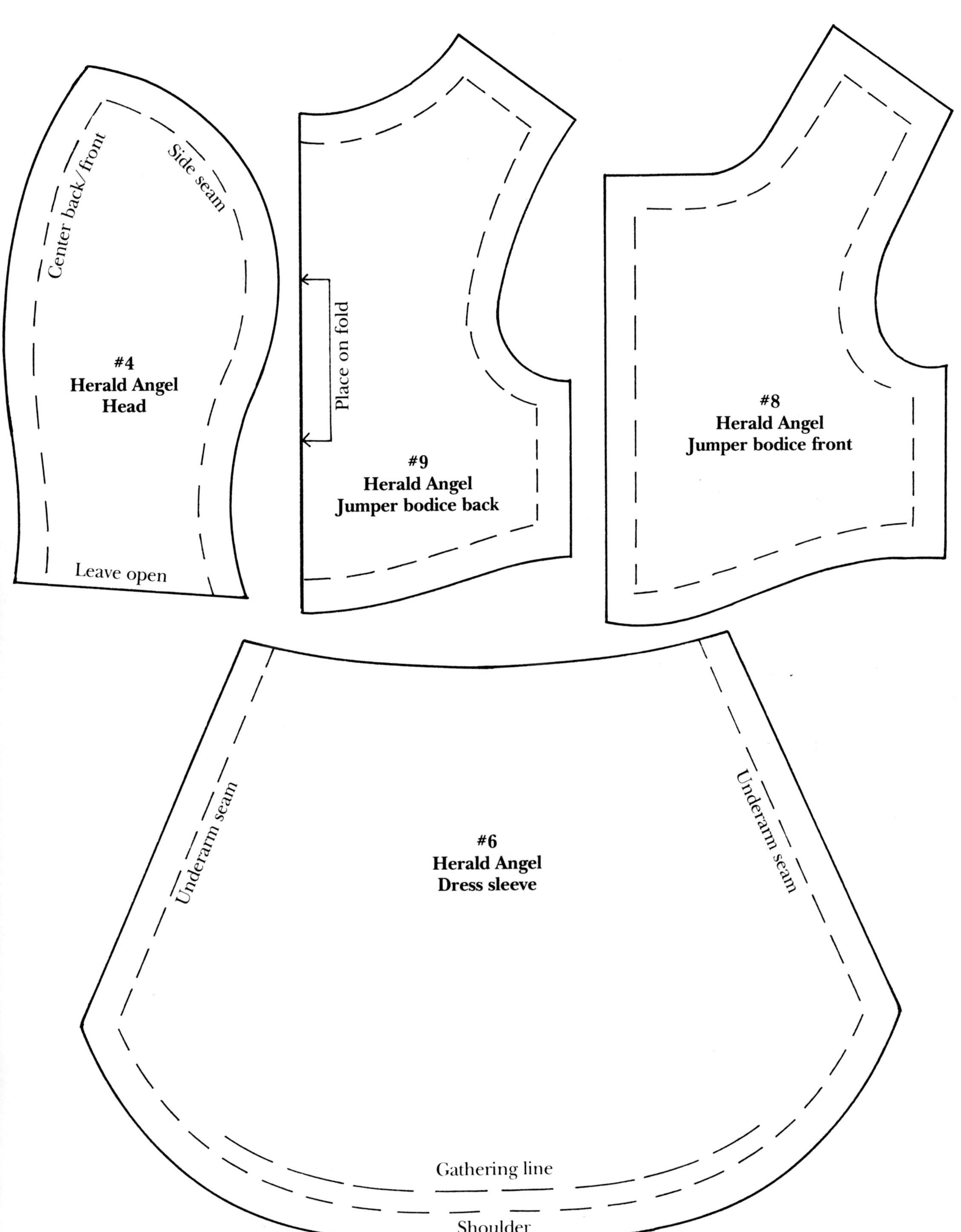
Center back/front
Side seam
#4
Herald Angel
Head
Leave open
Place on fold
#9
Herald Angel
Jumper bodice back
#8
Herald Angel
Jumper bodice front
Underarm seam
#6
Herald Angel
Dress sleeve
Underarm seam
Gathering line
Shoulder

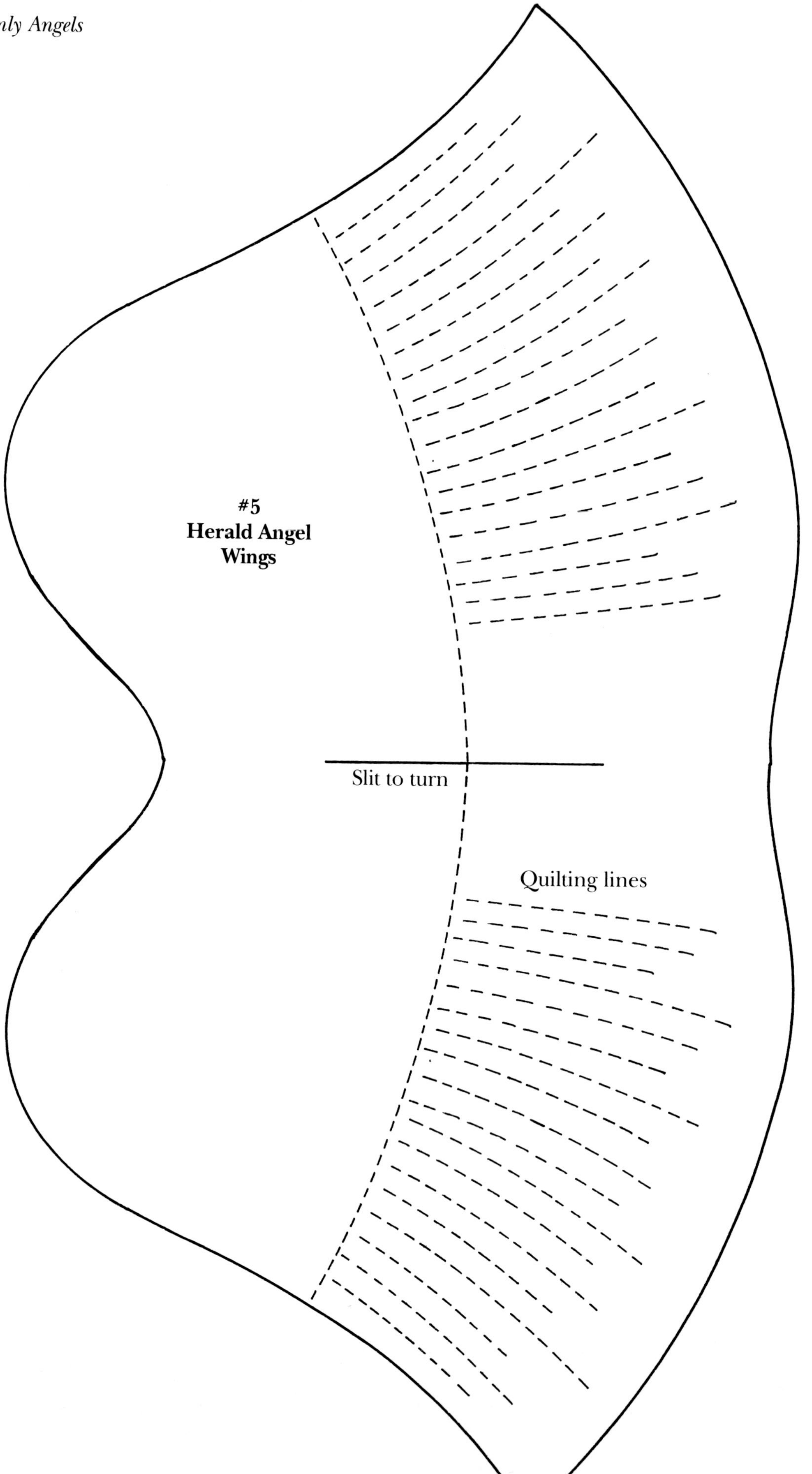

**#5
Herald Angel
Wings**

Slit to turn

Quilting lines

Snowstar

BRENT KANE

The Snowstar design was inspired by a wonderful scrap quilt that Kathleen Brassfield, my first quilting teacher years ago, designed and sewed. Kathleen has inspired me more than once! Both of these quilts share the same simple design, but are otherwise quite different. It is always amazing to me the route that inspiration can take and so much fun to see what you end up with.

CARL MURRAY

The Snowstar Quilt (above) is quick and easy to piece for a Christmas present. The angular edges of the six "star" segments add extra interest to the design in the Snowstar Tree Skirt (right).

Snowstar Quilt

60″ x 80″

You could easily make this quilt larger by adding six-inch borders all the way around. As is, it makes a great table cover!

MATERIALS

1½ yds. red
1½ yds. green
5½ yds. tan
3½ yds. fabric for backing
Batting

DIRECTIONS

1. Templates are found on large pull-out pattern sheet. Cut and piece 6 triangle units. Add small trapezoids. Following piecing diagram, sew to hexagons. Add diamonds to complete unit. Repeat for 5 more units. Sew center unit in same fashion, referring to photo for color changes.

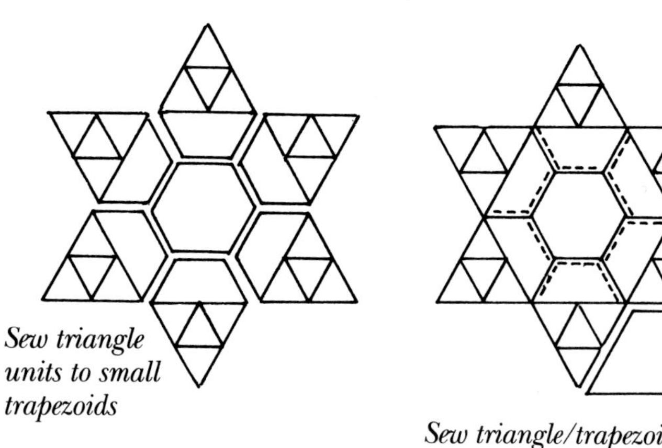

Sew triangle units to small trapezoids

Sew triangle/trapezoids to hexagon; add diamonds

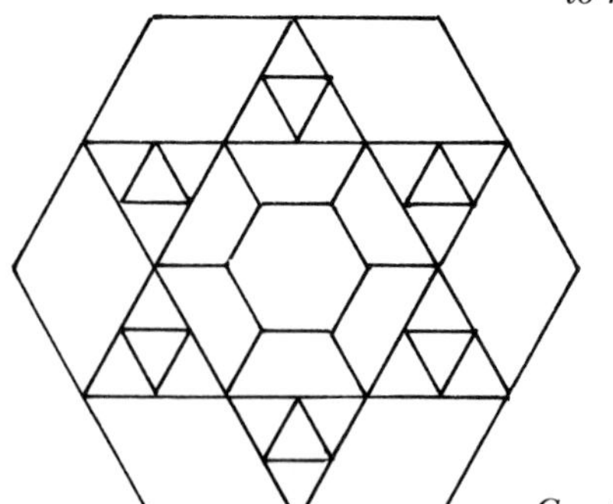

Completed hexagon unit

2. Sew 6 outer units to center unit. Following the cutting diagram, cut 4 large trapezoids and 6 half diamonds. Sew large trapezoids to the 4 corners and sew half diamonds to sides.

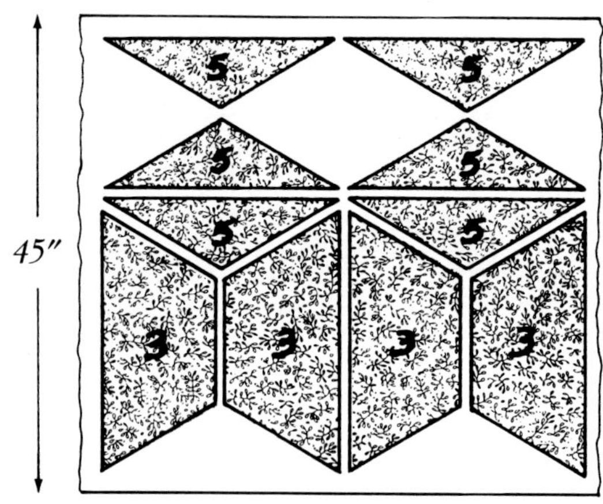

Cutting Diagram for Large Trapezoids and Half Diamonds

3. Cut 3 strips of tan 5⅝″ x 45″ (width of fabric) and sew end to end. From this, cut 2 strips 60″ long. Sew to top and bottom of quilt.
4. Piece 3 red and 2 green triangle units. Sew to medium trapezoids and add half trapezoids at each end. Sew to top of quilt. Repeat for bottom border.
5. Layer quilt with batting and backing. Tie quilt in center of hexagons, points of triangles, and in a triangular pattern on plain border strips and in large trapezoid areas.
6. Bind with green.

Piecing Diagram

Snowstar Tree Skirt

60″ x 63″

The inspiration for this design came from a quilt that Kathleen Brassfield recently made. You can also use this design to make a table cover by placing the triangle pattern at the top of the trapezoid pattern, creating a large triangle pattern for the center section.

MATERIALS

1¾ yds. red print for triangles and binding
1¾ yds. light print for triangles and diamonds
1½ yds. tan-and-white plaid for hexagons and center trapezoids
3⅔ yds. fabric for backing
Batting

DIRECTIONS

1. Templates are found on large pull-out pattern sheet. Cut and piece 6 triangle units and sew to hexagons. Piece in 6 diamonds. Sew a trapezoid to 1 side. Repeat to make 6 sections.

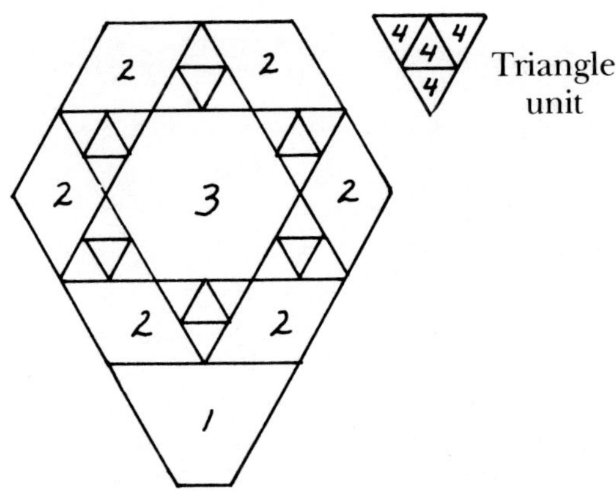

4 4 4 4
Triangle unit

2. Following piecing diagram, sew sections together, leaving 1 seam unsewn.
3. It will be necessary to seam both the backing fabric and the batting in order for them to be wide enough. Layer quilt with backing and batting and pin to hold. Cut backing and batting to same size as quilt. Tie quilt at corners of hexagons and at corners and centers of trapezoids.
4. Bind outside edge with red print. You will need approximately 226″ of binding. To bind the edges of the open sides, turn under the raw edges of the top and backing and slip-stitch together. To bind the center opening, cut binding 50″ long and leave a 15″ length of binding beyond both sides of the opening for tying. After binding, finish these 2 lengths by pressing raw edges together and sewing along the open side and across the bottom of each.

Open

Piecing Diagram

Family Fun

Add to your Christmas decor with the We're All Together Quilt, Reindeer and Sleigh soft sculpture, and My Favorite Things Ornaments.

CARL MURRAY

Christmas is a time for families. The We're All Together quilt was designed two years ago when our family wasn't all together for the very first time. Our daughter Jenny was in California with her husband and five-month-old, Duncan. We all hated it and my husband, Jim, swore that, by the time he paid all of the phone bills, he could have flown them home and back. The Reindeer and Sleigh remind me of my gramma's house, where family traditions begin in my memory. I can still recall the cozy feeling of being under her big dining room table, while legs rushed to and fro getting a holiday dinner ready.

We're All Together Quilt

14½″ x 27½″

MATERIALS

12″ x 15″, 14 ct. ivory Aida
⅜ yd. berry red for center background
¼ yd. medium-dark green for upper and lower background
⅛ yd. each of 6 brown prints and solids for reindeer
⅛ yd. black for antlers
⅛ yd. muslin for 1 set of antlers
¼ yd. dark brown for border and binding
½ yd. fabric for backing
Batting
Green, red, and light brown embroidery floss (see chart)

DIRECTIONS

1. From the Aida, cut 2 strips 1½″ x 13″. Cross-stitch center motif on remaining piece, using chart on page 61 as a guide to stitching and color placement. Machine stay-stitch 15 squares from edge of design on all 4 sides. Cut fabric evenly all the way around, leaving 10 squares beyond stay-stitching.
2. Cut red center square 13″ x 13″. Fold into quarters to find center lines. Fold cross-stitch in same fashion. Lay cross-stitch on red square, matching up fold lines; pin. Using a running stitch and 2 strands of green floss, sew cross-stitch fabric to red square along machine stitching.
3. Cut 2 green background pieces 7″ x 13″. Using pattern pieces on page 62, cut out and position appliques on background fabric, noting correct sequence in diagrams on page 62; applique. The easiest way to achieve correct placement for the appliques is to study the photograph and determine which templates need to be cut for each reindeer. You may add more reindeer, both small and large, as fits your family. The reindeer with the muslin antlers is the great-gramma of the family.
4. Sew Aida strips to appliqued fabric. Sew to top and bottom of center square. Cut 2 brown strips 1½″ x 13″ and 2 brown strips 1½″ x 28″. Sew shorter strips to top and bottom of quilt and longer strips to sides.
5. Layer quilt with batting and backing. Outline quilt around appliques and ⅛″ from border seams.
6. Bind with brown.

My Favorite Things Ornaments

3″–4″ tall

These look attractive around windows and doorways or mixed in with a swag of greens.

MATERIALS

⅛ yd. red print
⅛ yd. green print
⅛ yd. white print
5 yds. cream satin ribbon, 1/16″ wide
Batting

DIRECTIONS

1. Pattern pieces are on large pull-out pattern sheet. Using the Flat Sculpture method described on page 9, sew 2 of each shape, mixing the fabric colors as desired.
2. Thread a large-eyed needle with a 7½″ length of ribbon, which has been knotted at 1 end. Sew through shape from back to front and knot the long end close to the shape. Repeat for each shape until each has 2 ribbons sewn on. Tie ribbons together into bows for individual ornaments or tie shapes together for garland.

Reindeer and Sleigh

4″ tall x 32″ long

This decoration reminds me of the celluloid reindeer and cardboard sleigh my Gramma always had on her mantel. Sparkles were glued on them, and, try as I might, I couldn't keep from picking them up. I never could figure out how Gramma knew I'd been holding them.

MATERIALS

⅛ yd. red plaid for reindeer
⅛ yd. red print for reindeer
⅛ yd. red solid for reindeer
⅛ yd. green print for reindeer
⅛ yd. green solid for sleigh
Polyester stuffing
28″ jute twine, 3-ply
2⅔ yds. cream satin ribbon, 1/16″ wide
Glue gun

DIRECTIONS

1. Assemble 8 reindeer and 2 sleighs, using trace, stitch, and cut technique (see page 9). Pattern pieces are on page 60. Sew entire outlines, except leave reindeer heads open as indicated for antlers.
2. Pair up reindeer colors as desired and lay them facing each other. Cut a 2″ opening for turning through only 1 fabric layer in each pair. Make sure that the cut is on the opposite side of each pair.
3. Turn and stuff firmly. Slip-stitch openings closed.
4. Cut eight 3½″ lengths of jute. Fold in half. Insert fold into reindeer's head; glue opening. Fray jute down ¾″ and glue to prevent further fraying.
5. Stand reindeer pairs next to each other, slightly leaning together, and one ahead of the other by ½″. Glue together in this position. Repeat for other 3 pairs and sleigh.
6. Cut two 48″ lengths of ribbon. Thread a needle with the ribbon and tie a knot in 1 end. Start on the left side of the pairs and sew ribbon through the nose of the first reindeer, with knot to the inside. Knot ribbon on the outside close to the nose. Make another knot 8″ from the outside knot and sew ribbon again through the second reindeer nose. Again, knot ribbon on the outside. Repeat for third and fourth reindeers and sleigh, leaving 8″ each time between knots. Tie excess ribbon on the outside of the sleigh in a bow. Repeat for the right side.

REINDEER AND SLEIGH

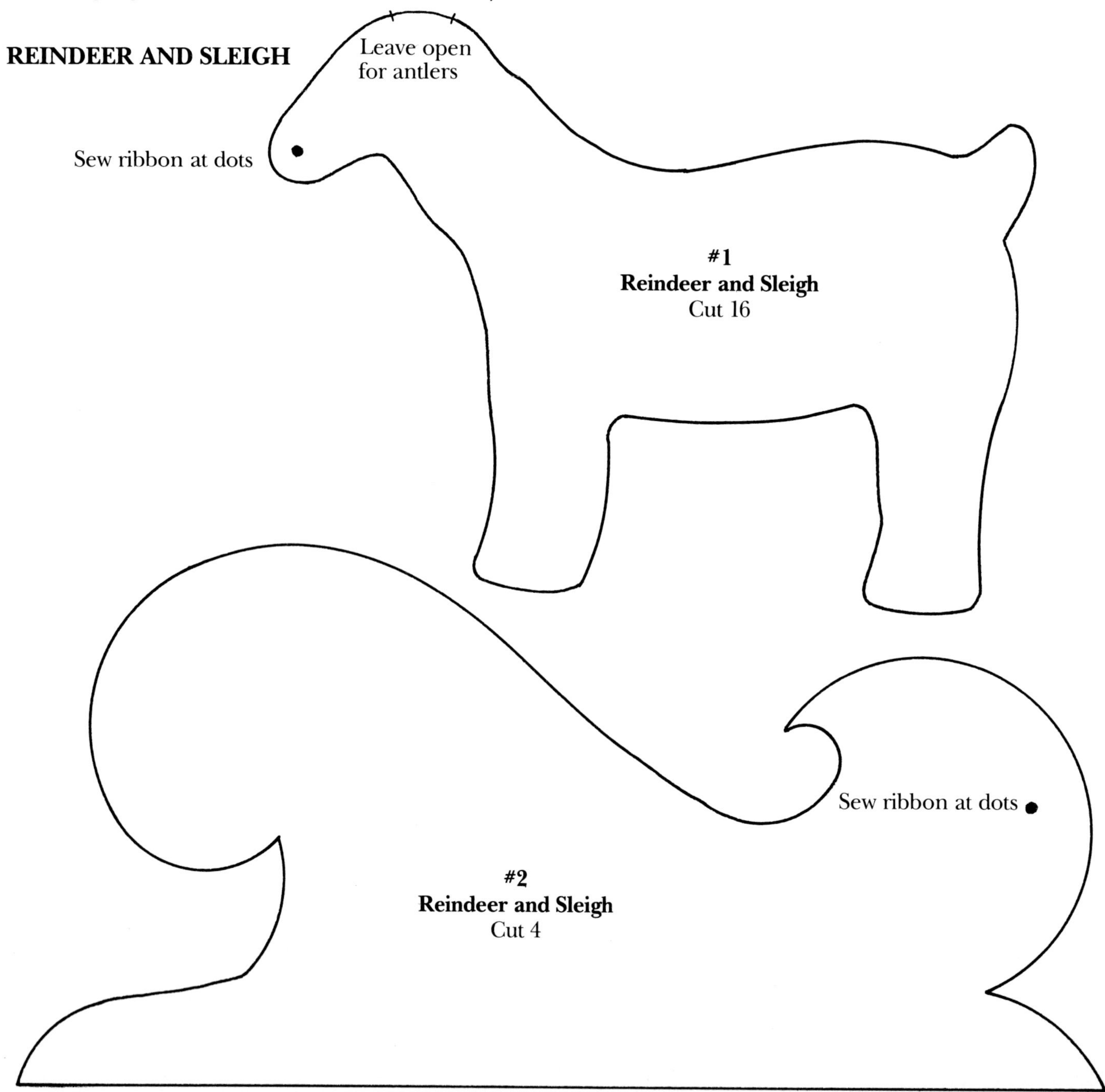

WE'RE ALL TOGETHER QUILT

DMC	COLOR
× 221	Dark red
◊ 407	Medium copper
▲ 501	Dark green

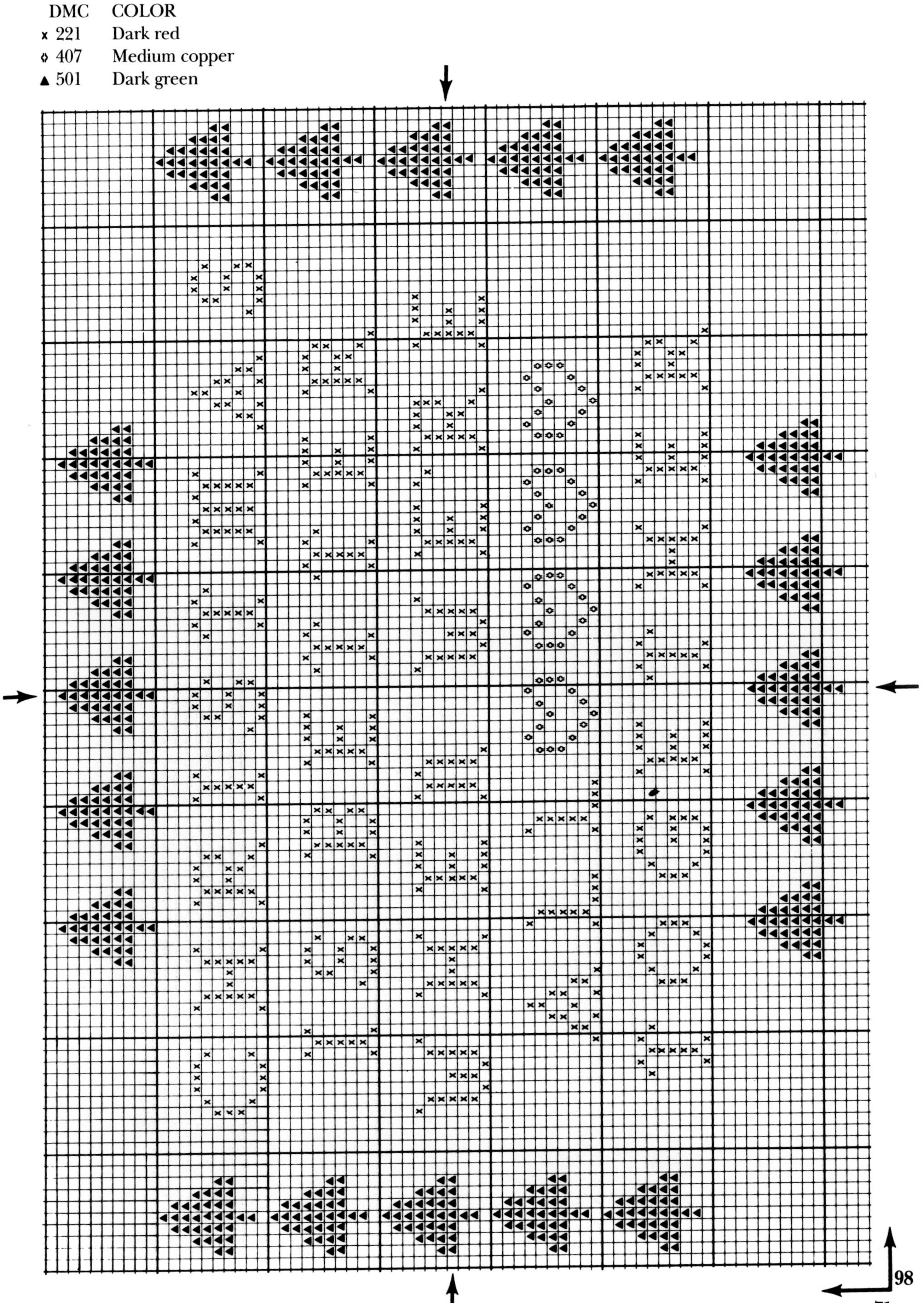

Placement Sequence Diagram (top motif)

Placement Sequence Diagram (bottom motif)

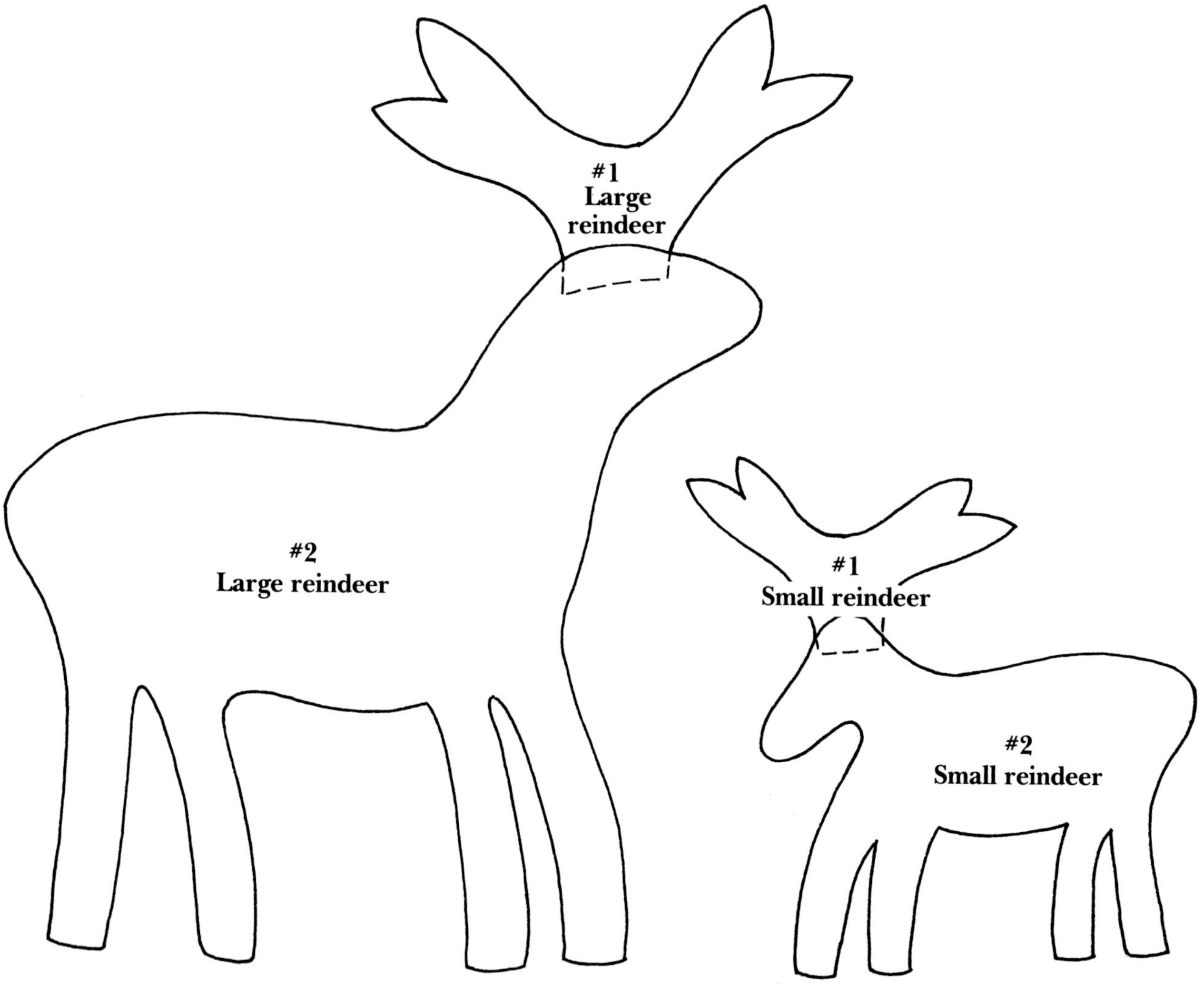

#1 Large reindeer

#2 Large reindeer

#1 Small reindeer

#2 Small reindeer

Sharing with Children

CARL MURRAY

Our fondest memories of Christmases past have nothing to do with the gifts any of us received. Invariably, we talk about the year we made all of the stockings, or the year each of the kids managed to spill the cookie decorations at least three times, or the year the Christmas tree fell on Gramma, who was sleeping on the hideabed. These are the times the kids remember, when we were all together doing something special.

Many of the projects in this section will keep children busy as you prepare for the Holidays. The Prairie Tree Quilt is simple enough for a beginning quilter and could even be appliqued and signed by several stitchers for their favorite relative. Even a preschooler could make Spice Ornaments from felt and stitch them up. Angel the Cat should earn a smile from any true cat fancier and will gladly share the season with any doll or animal lucky enough to have Extra Angel Wings made just for them! And wouldn't Grampa be proud of the Bookmark his granddaughter made?

These projects are designed to keep small hands busy during family gatherings or hectic holiday preparations. From left to right: Angel the Cat, Spice Ornaments, Prairie Tree Quilt, and Bookmarks. A Button Garland is in front.

Prairie Tree Quilt

10½″ x 15″

MATERIALS

⅛ yd. navy check for trees
⅛ yd. navy plaid for trees
⅛ yd. navy flower for trees and border
⅛ yd. muslin for tree
⅛ yd. navy print for background
⅛ yd. tan solid for background
⅓ yd. fabric for backing

DIRECTIONS

1. Using pattern pieces on page 66, cut out 12 appliques and 12 background pieces. Applique trees onto background fabric.
2. Sew squares together, referring to photograph for placement.
3. Cut 2 strips 2″ x 12½″ from border fabric and sew to sides of quilt. Cut 2 strips 2″ x 11″ and sew to top and bottom of quilt.
4. Finish quilt with a No-Bind backing (see page 8 for instructions).

Spice Ornaments

2″ and 3″ tall

MATERIALS

Small pieces of old quilt or heavy flannel
Newly purchased cans of whole cloves and/or allspice or any other favorite whole spices
Button thread, either matching or contrasting
Stuffing (optional)

DIRECTIONS

1. Using pattern pieces on page 66, cut out 2 of each shape, reversing as necessary to make a set. Do not add seam allowance.
2. Pin with wrong sides together. Sew with a buttonhole stitch, leaving an opening to insert spices. Fill with spices until slightly rounded, not bulging. Sew opening closed.
3. If you are using a lighter-weight fabric, you may wish to add a small amount of stuffing before adding the spices.
4. Your choice of thread color and the quality of your stitches can give these either a fine hand-worked look or a "little girl" primitive look. The easiest way to achieve the primitive look is with black thread and irregular stitches. You can even throw in a few running stitches. For a nicely finished look, use a closely matching thread and even stitches. This would be a fun place to try out some additional decorative stitches.

Angel the Cat

5¾″ and 9″ tall

Angel is named for our indoors cat with the most seniority, but it really reminds me of a cat, named Pinky, I had when I was growing up. Pinky suffered through several years of my putting doll's dresses on him with very little complaint, and I am sure he is an angel somewhere now!

MATERIALS

⅛ yd. camel Osnaburg cloth for body (can be dyed, if desired—see page 6 for dyeing tips)
¼ yd. print for gown
⅛ yd. small checkerboard prints for wings
Black and ecru embroidery floss
Polyester stuffing
Batting for wings
Fabric glue

DIRECTIONS

1. Pattern pieces are on pages 67–69. Assemble body/head, 2 arms, and 2 legs, using trace, stitch, and cut technique (see page 9); stuff. Slip-stitch openings closed. Position top edge of legs and arms ¼″ behind body seam. Sew on with a blind stitch.
2. With a single strand each of black and ecru floss, sew whiskers. Knot whiskers close to fabric to keep from pulling out. You can use the same 2 strands of floss to make French knots for the eyes.
3. Cut gown from print fabric. Sew shoulder, underarm, and side seams. Clip corners and turn to right side.
4. Turn down neck seam and sew with 2 strands of ecru floss and a long running stitch, leaving a 4″ tail to the

outside at the beginning and end of the hem. You can then draw up the neck opening and tie the ends in a bow, when the gown is put on the cat.

5. Turn under sleeves ¼″ and hem. Turn under lower edge of gown ½″ and hem. These hems need be only running stitches.
6. For wings: Cut 3 strips from checkerboard print fabrics 2″ x 9″ (for larger wings) or 1½″ wide x 6″ (for smaller wings). Sew the strips together lengthwise and press seams. Fold with right sides together and sew with batting as for Flat Sculpture (see page 9). Glue to gown.

Button Garland

36″ long

I have a hard time passing up jars of old buttons at antique shops. This attraction to old buttons, I am sure, comes from my childhood. I remember spending many hours at Gramma's, stringing buttons onto a piece of yarn. I loved going through those buttons, sorting the colors and making necklaces for Gramma and me. She would proudly wear those necklaces all day.

I have accumulated a large collection of old mother-of-pearl buttons, which I love to use on dolls and other projects. It is always fun going through them to sort out the ones I want to use. Think of the history in those jars!

This simple decoration is perfect for little miniature trees, and children old enough to use a needle can easily make these. Make sure you provide children with a blunt or rounded tapestry needle so they will not prick their fingers.

MATERIALS

Cream-colored cotton crochet thread
#5 cotton darning needle (with blunt end)
Old mother-of-pearl buttons (about 42)

DIRECTIONS

Thread needle with a 60″ length of crochet thread. Bring needle up through 1 hole in a button and pull thread through until about 5″ of thread remains. Tie a knot at the top of the button and thread on another button. Tie it about ¾″ from the first. Repeat until there is only about 5″ left. Tie the ends in a slipknot to secure them to the tree.

Extra Angel Wings

If your house is like mine, there are probably several of your favorite stuffed bears, rabbits, cats, or dolls who deserve to wear wings at Christmas. For this reason, I have included some additional patterns for angel wings on page 70. These are marked "Extra angel wings" and are sewn as for Flat Sculpture (see page 9). Just add ribbons and tie them onto those who are the most deserving!

Bookmarks

2″ x 5½″ and 2″ x 6½″

These could also be done on cross-stitch fabric.

MATERIALS

Strips of perforated paper cut to size
Embroidery floss
½ yd. of 2″ wide red or green ribbon

DIRECTIONS

1. Using 3 strands of embroidery floss and following chart on page 71 for stitching and color placement, complete cross-stitch design. With 2 strands of embroidery floss, finish edge with a running stitch in the second row of holes from the edge.
2. Cut 8″ and 10″ lengths of ribbon. Glue paper to ribbon, leaving 1″ of ribbon extending beyond paper.

Snow Angel

I haven't seen this done lately, but I can't imagine that the art is dying out. For those who may have forgotten the technique: Dress one small child in training pants, undershirt, T-shirt, overalls, socks, and shoes. Then add snow pants, coat, boots, mittens, and hat. Undress quickly and run to the nearest bathroom. Put on dry training pants and overalls. Repeat as above. Dress yourself in like fashion.

Go outside and locate the smoothest patch of fresh snow. Lay child in snow. Lie down yourself. Swing arms through snow in an arc from head to legs. Swing legs out slightly.

Carefully stand up and help child to stand. Enjoy the look of pure delight on child's face!

Recipes

When the kids were all small, the snowbound days we spent stuck in the house were special days. We celebrated with a traditional "fresh snow" lunch of popcorn, Snow Ice Cream, and Russian Tea. This "well-balanced meal" was usually eaten on the living room floor surrounded by blocks, dolls, and books.

SNOW ICE CREAM

2 eggs
2 cups milk
½ tsp. salt
3 tsp. vanilla
1½ cups sugar
Clean snow, about 6 qts.

Beat eggs till lemon-colored; add milk, salt, vanilla, and sugar. Beat in snow, until of ice cream consistency.

RUSSIAN TEA

4 cinnamon sticks
14 whole allspice
12 whole cloves
9 tea bags
Juice of 1 lemon
1 large can orange drink
1 large can pineapple drink
1 cup sugar, or to taste

In a covered pot, simmer cinnamon, allspice, and cloves with tea bags in 2 quarts of water for 10 minutes. Add lemon juice, orange and pineapple drinks, and sugar. Heat till warm.

We like to keep this simmering on the back of the stove so that it's ready to warm us up when we come in from outside. It will also do well in a crock pot. Since the kids have grown up, we cut back on the sugar and use grapefruit juice in place of the sweeter drinks.

SPICE ORNAMENTS

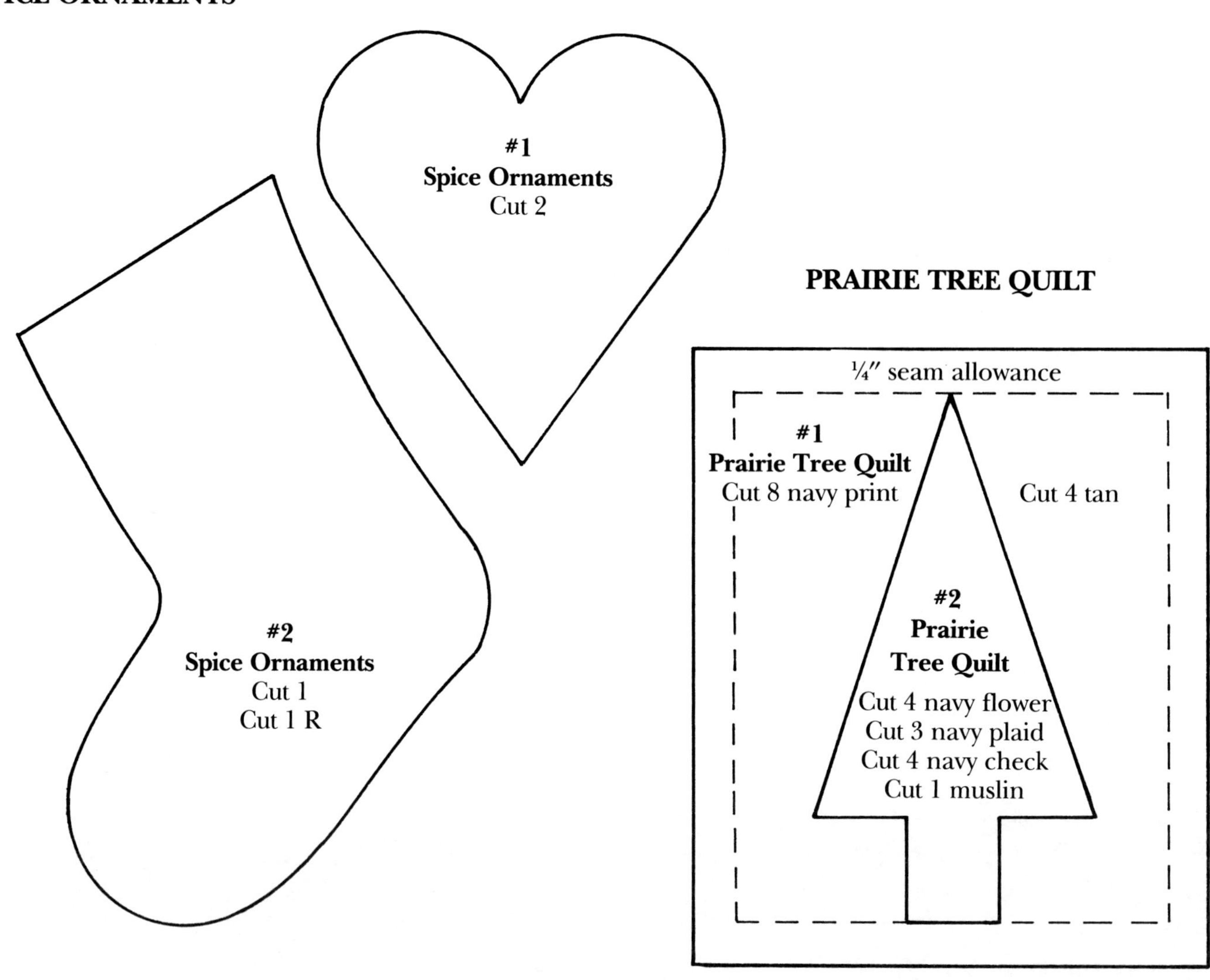

ANGEL THE CAT

#5
Angel the Cat 9″
Gown

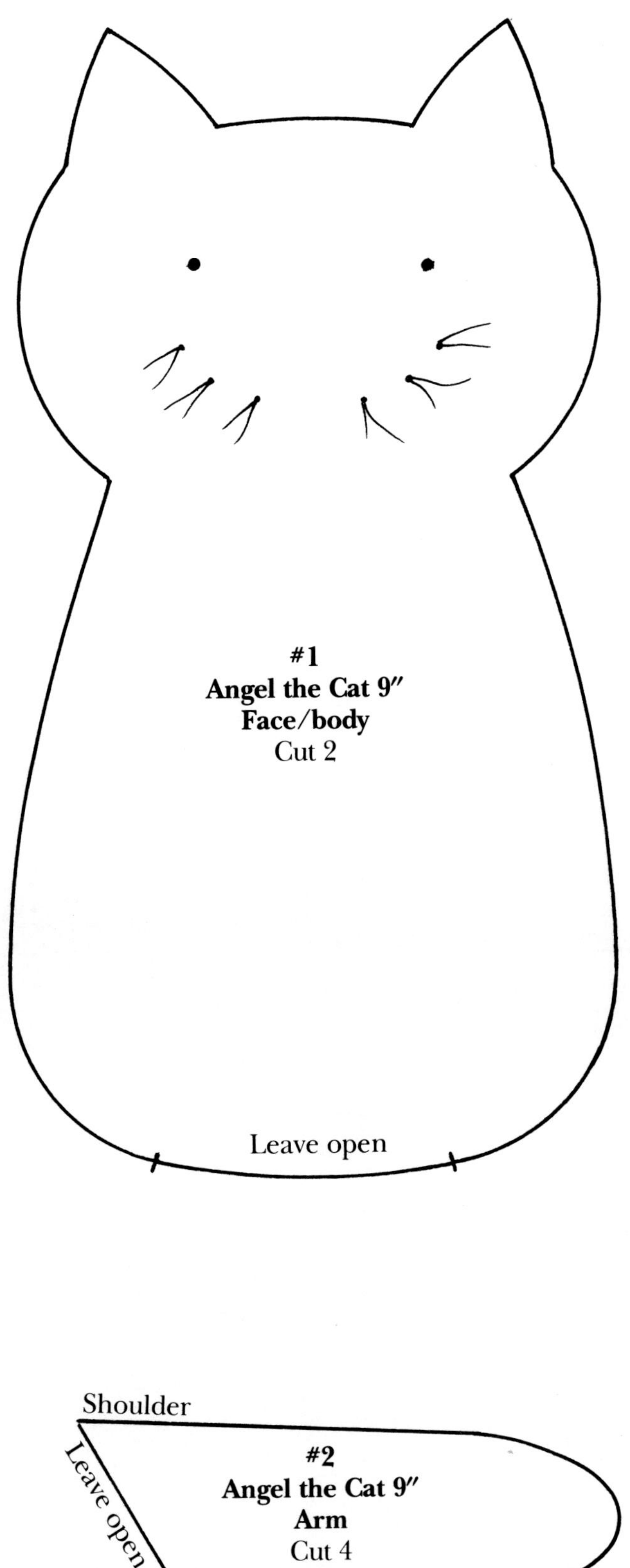
#1
Angel the Cat 9″
Face/body
Cut 2
Leave open
Shoulder
Leave open
#2
Angel the Cat 9″
Arm
Cut 4

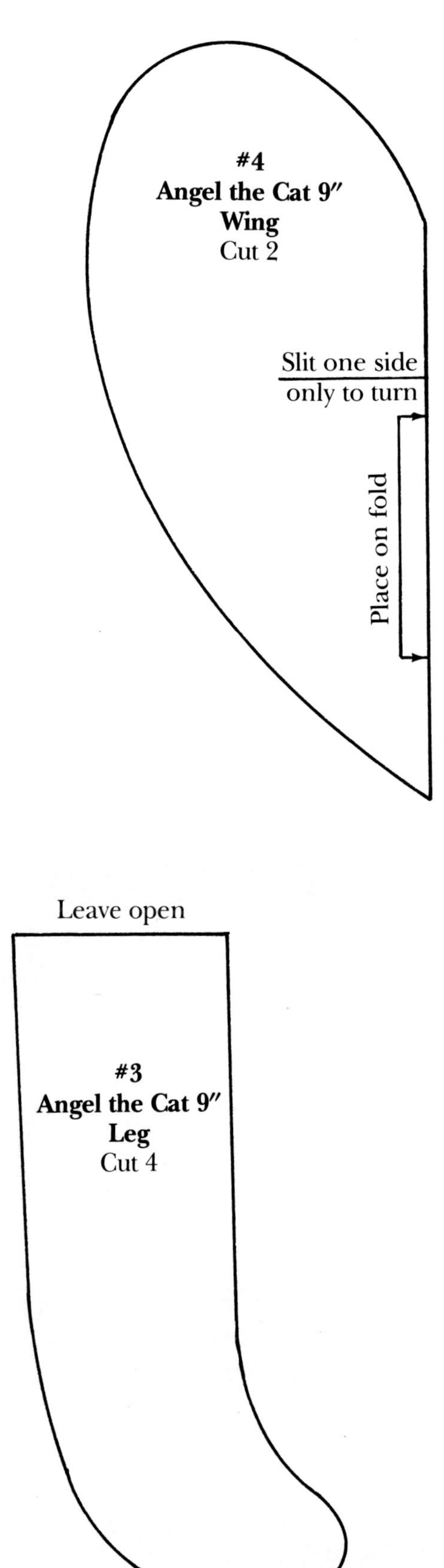
#4
Angel the Cat 9″
Wing
Cut 2
Slit one side
only to turn
Place on fold
Leave open
#3
Angel the Cat 9″
Leg
Cut 4

EXTRA ANGEL WINGS

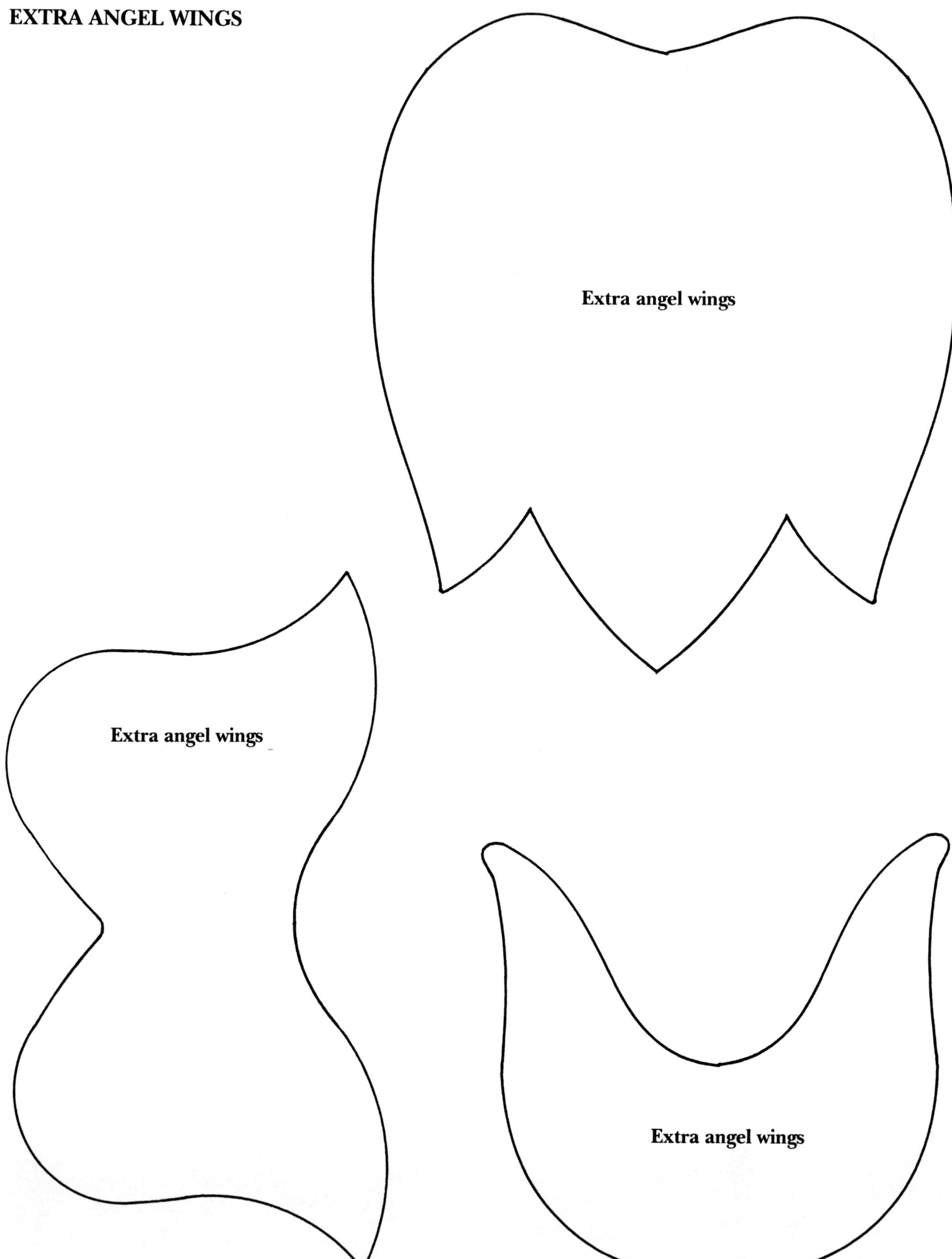

BOOKMARKS

	DMC	COLOR
●	822	White
♥	501	Dark green
★	221	Dark red
#	776	Pink

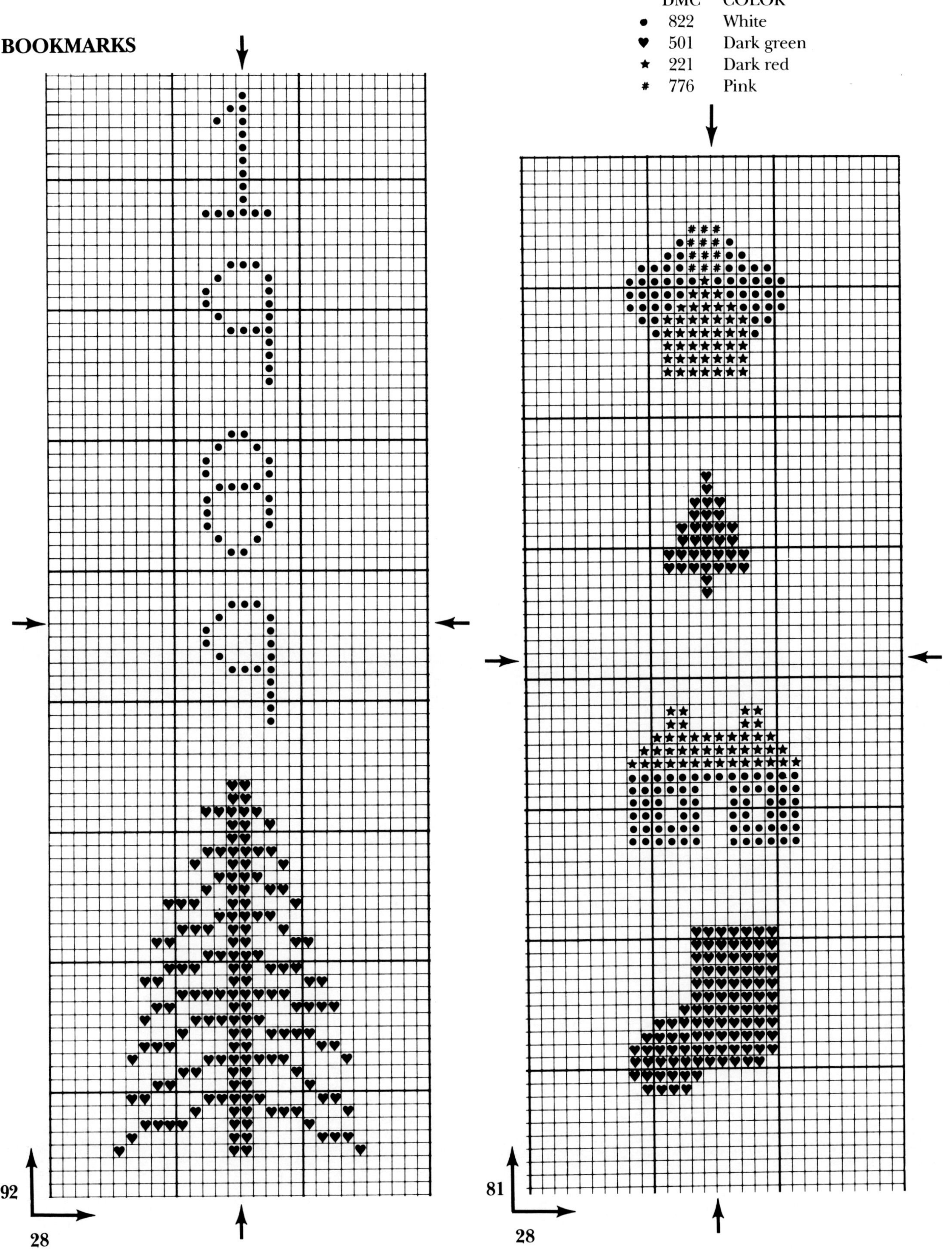

That Patchwork Place Publications

Baby Quilts from Grandma by Carolann Palmer
Back to Square One by Nancy J. Martin
A Banner Year by Nancy J. Martin
Christmas Memories—A Folk Art Celebration by Nancy J. Martin
Copy Art for Quilters by Nancy J. Martin
A Dozen Variables by Marsha McCloskey and Nancy J. Martin
Even More by Trudie Hughes
Feathered Star Quilts by Marsha McCloskey
Feathered Star Sampler by Marsha McCloskey
Happy Endings—Finishing the Edges of Your Quilt by Mimi Dietrich
Holiday Happenings by Christal Carter
Housing Projects by Nancy J. Martin
Little By Little: Quilts in Miniature by Mary Hickey
More Template-Free Quiltmaking by Trudie Hughes
My Mother's Quilts: Designs from the Thirties by Sara Nephew
One-of-a-Kind Quilts by Judy Hopkins
Pieces of the Past by Nancy J. Martin
Projects for Blocks and Borders by Marsha McCloskey
Reflections of Baltimore by Jeana Kimball
Small Quilts by Marsha McCloskey
Template-Free Quiltmaking by Trudie Hughes
Women and Their Quilts: A Washington State Centennial Tribute by Nancyann Johanson Twelker

For more information, send $2 for a color catalog to That Patchwork Place, Inc., P.O. Box 118, Bothell, WA 98041-0118. Many titles are available at your local quilt shop.